TWO WEEKS STRAIT

HOW TO SUCCEED WHEN YOUR HANDS ARE TIED

Brad,

THANK you so MUCH
FOR your HELP ONSTAGE.
You WERE AMAZING!

MARK CLEARVIEW

Proceeds from this book will benefit the Michael J. Fox Foundation for Parkinson's Research

 FriesenPress

One Printers Way
Altona, MB RoG oBo
Canada

www.friesenpress.com

Content edited by
Erik Berg
Madelyn Keys

Copy edited by
Juliann Garisto

Cover design by
Brandon James

With help from
Adriana Bogaard
Rosemary Reid
Max Litzgus

This book is a memoir. It reflects the author's present recollections of experiences over time. Some names and characteristics have been changed, some events have been compressed, and some dialogue has been recreated.

ISBN
978-1-03-913459-1 (Hardcover)
978-1-03-913458-4 (Paperback)
978-1-03-913460-7 (eBook)

1. HUMOR, CELEBRITY & POPULAR CULTURE

Distributed to the trade by The Ingram Book Company

A note about the editors:

Erik Berg is an actor, writer, and director. Born and raised in the West End of Winnipeg, he later appeared in over ten television and film productions (such as *The Haunting in Connecticut* and *More Than Meets the Eye*), subsequently graduating from the National Theatre School. Berg co-wrote and starred in the internationally acclaimed movie, *88:88*. He currently lives in Toronto where he works on filmmaking and poetry.

Madelyn Keys is an award-winning writer, director, and up-and-coming actor. Originally from Ottawa, Canada, Keys has been working consistently across film and television for the past twelve years. She strives to tell stories of perseverance, often working with topics such as mental health, LGBTQ+ issues, and coming-of-age stories.

Juliann Garisto is a writer and editor. She was born and raised in Toronto and continues to reside there as prose editor for the *Hart House Review*, an annual Canadian literary magazine. Garisto recently graduated with a BA in English and Philosophy from the University of Toronto, and is hoping to get her MA in Creative Writing. Her favourite author is Elena Ferrante.

Dedicated to Michael J. Fox,
the ten million people living with Parkinson's disease,
and everyone who shared the love throughout.

TABLE OF CONTENTS

LIVE TELEVISION

JULY 28, 2014: Staggering in a haze, I look around the television studio. Cameras fixed on me, focusing. My heart pounding. This was the moment I'd been waiting for. I down some protein powder while the crew hastily attaches a microphone to my belt. Everyone takes their position. Mine is a small piece of spike tape pressed into the floor, centre stage. *The Morning Show* host begins counting down: *"We're live in three, two—"*

I can't do this.

A camera operator points at me, and the intro music begins to play. Suddenly we're live. Although the hosts continue talking, I don't hear another word. Maybe they make some jokes about how I smell. I don't remember.

Go for it?

I start squirming, accomplishing nothing. Two minutes left?

I search my body for a morsel of energy, knowing that if I can't find it, I won't have the time to escape.

What are my options? Apologize? Collapse? Vomit?

No. Get out.

Adrenaline. Finally. I jerk my body back and forth. Get out. My brain screaming now, *"Get out!"*

July 28, 2014: My first out-of-body experience. Like I'm standing in the audience with my friends and family, looking back at my straitjacket-bound body. Watching, smiling, waiting, and quietly wondering: How the hell did I end up here?

TALKING THE TALK

(Centre of Attention: My first time doing standup—1998)

What? The first chapter ends on a cliffhanger?

First of all, I'll use whatever rhetorical devices I damn well please, and second: if you really want to know how the story ends, you can jump straight to the last page and break the trust of this budding relationship. But there's nothing worse than ruining a good thing by moving too fast. So, let's get to know each other first, yeah?

When I was eighteen, I spent two weeks strapped in a straitjacket to raise money for Parkinson's disease research. Video blogging every day.

No tricks, no freedom, and no breaks. I called it Escaping Parkinson's, and at the end of my two weeks, I planned to … well, escape.

Since those suffering from Parkinson's don't have that option, I was hoping that with the money raised we'd be one step closer to escaping Parkinson's. Which you'll realize is the name of the … you understand.

This is a story about how I spent fourteen days in a straitjacket, and how that experience changed my life. And while I'm writing this with hopes of inspiring you, I must admit that I'm going through this process to find answers myself. Like, what was pushing me toward success? Why didn't I quit? Did I make the impact I'd hoped? And how did I go to the bathroom? Let's buckle up and find out.[1]

SOMETIME IN LATE 2010: I'm sitting across from a world-renowned escape artist in a cafe outside of Oakville, Ontario. How did I end up there? Where's Oakville? What's an Ontario?[2] Perhaps we'll start earlier.

In the beginning there was God, and God created light, and He saw that the light was good.

Too early?

---

1 Pun intended.

2 It's in Canada, you ignorant slob.

Somewhere down the road, I was born. I grew up in a small town just outside of Toronto.[3] It's important to mention that I was born Mark *Correia*. Clearview is a stage name I adopted after all this. In the interest of clarity and accuracy to the story, I will be sticking with *Correia* from now on. I was *Correia* then, and I'm *Correia* in this book, dammit! At my third birthday party, I saw a magician and fell in love with magic. I started practicing magic when I was four years old, performing for audiences when I was five, and professionally entertaining (for money) when I was six.[4]

My parents also divorced that year (remaining close friends), so it was win/lose. I lived mainly at my mom's, but visited my dad every other day, so they both come up a lot in therapy. My mom and dad were always supportive of my passion for creating wonder and laughter for strangers. My parents liked seeing me happy, I guess, because they never stopped me from doing it (yes, even people whose parents supported them need therapy sometimes).

An interest in acting followed. I figured that if I wanted to do good magic, I had to do good acting. Every self-proclaimed magician who can find your card more than half the time will tell you: *"A magician is an actor playing the part of a magician,"* because a very prolific magician named Robert-Houdin said it over two hundred years ago. But I'm better than those magicians, so I won't mention it.

Eventually, I developed an unhealthy obsession with being the centre of attention, something my parents weren't so supportive of. Call it "only child syndrome," my ADHD, or my heart being two sizes too small—whatever it was, it got me into serious trouble. More importantly than serious trouble, it got me into comedy.[5] I try to work humour into every-

---

3 Oakville. It's actually a big town, big enough to be a city. Small town just sounds better.

4 I've only ever done magic since. I've never worked another job. Really.

5 If you can't tell that I have an interest in comedy by now, stop reading.

thing that I do, and besides, everything is more fun when you're laughing. It's a scientific fact!

When I was twelve years old, I landed a gig opening for another magician at a gala event. I did some store-bought tricks and delivered some poorly written jokes before it was his turn to take the stage. *"Ladies and gentlemen, please welcome two-time Guinness World Record holding magician, Scott Hammell."*[6] Scott took the stage and performed thirty minutes of what I was sure was the greatest performance ever. Then he took out the straitjacket that made him famous. Two volunteers tied him up so tight that I became vicariously uncomfortable. He then launched his body around the stage for five excruciating minutes. When he finally freed himself, the entire crowd leapt to their feet. Never before had I seen a straitjacket escape, a performer of this calibre, and honestly, a standing ovation.

After the show, Scott showered my act with praise (although I'm not sure why) and signed my program:

"Mark, you'll be breaking my records one day! Call me if you need anything."

- Scott Hammell

When I got home, I looked up those records. *2003:* The Highest Suspension Straitjacket Escape. He was strapped into a regulation straitjacket and dangled 7,200 feet in the air from a hot air balloon. He escaped. *2006:* Longest Inverted Juggling. He hung upside down and juggled by throwing the balls towards his feet for just under two minutes.

But the overachiever has done more since then: *2009:* World's Fastest Moving Card Trick. He caught a chosen playing card in mid-air while skydiving. What?

2010: Highest Blindfolded Skydive. He jumped out of an airplane in handcuffs and escaped just in time to pull his ripcord. He'd bet a group

---

6 He is now four-time Guinness World Record holding magician Scott Hammell.

of high school students that if he could do the stunt, they would raise enough money to build a school in Ecuador. He did. They did.

All this time Scott was afraid of heights. As you've probably noticed, he's made a bit of a habit of facing his fears and creating positive change— but he can write more about that in his own book. Long story short, I was inspired to all hell. You might think this leads right into the story of how we met, but I was too nervous to contact Scott as a twelve-year-old boy. It would have to wait … for now.

When I was fourteen, I started to pursue acting more seriously. I auditioned for and was accepted into the Etobicoke School of the Arts Drama program. I met my closest friends at ESA. How lucky was I to find like-minded people? It's hard to think of anything more important than friendship. Without that, we end up relying on ourselves, and that's where we get some of our worst advice.

My friend group called themselves the "Kool Kats," which was much cooler in high school, I promise.[7] ESA helped me gain more confidence in myself as an artist, and I began performing more regularly. As performances picked up, I began booking out the theatre at my school to develop more original material. While practicing some physical comedy in front of the mirror one day, I came up with an idea. What about adding a straitjacket escape to my own act? eBay was where you went for literally anything at the time. I purchased a straitjacket after doing very little research and was shocked when it arrived without escape instructions.[8] I grabbed the program Scott had signed two years earlier from a shoebox tucked away in the back corner of my closet and dialled the number (on a freaking landline). A shy twelve-year-old no longer, I began to grill Scott

---

7 It wasn't.

8 This now makes perfect sense to me.

on the specifics of his escape. Shockingly, he replied: *"Let's meet up. I'll show you!"*

Enough background? I'm fourteen years old, sometime in late 2010, waiting for a world-renowned magician in a coffee shop outside of my hometown with a straitjacket in my backpack. Not strange at all.

He arrived carrying this big brown case. *"So nice to see you, man!"* he said, with genuine enthusiasm in his smile. He threw the mysterious case onto the table.

We began speaking and looking over the jacket that I had just ordered, before Scott said, *"Here, let's look at a real straitjacket."* He clicked his case open to reveal a regulation Posey brand jacket. I vividly remember holding it—the rough textured surface, the cold metal buckles. I was struck by how heavy and ominous the real thing was.

"So why do you want to learn this escape?" Scott asked.

Before I could tell him anything about my new show he said, *"You should set a world record!"* Uh yeah, why not?[9]

But how?

We started spitballing ideas during our first ever meeting until we were just laughing and saying stupid stuff like, *"Hey, what about the world's slowest straitjacket escape?"*

Scott has been my mentor and friend since that day.

In addition to planting the seed for my stunt, Scott also played a significant role in shaping my career. He is one of the all-around greatest humans you could know, and the fact that he was willing to meet before I had anything to offer and only everything to gain (from him) tells you a lot about who he is.

---

9 I wish I had the naïveté of my fourteen-year-old self.

After some lessons with Scott in my school's black-box theatre, the escape became the closer in my act. People ask if escaping a straitjacket is a magic trick. Not really. It's a learnable skill and is more about technique than secrecy. Everyone who performs it has a different method for escaping, and the methods range from trick jackets to shoulder dislocation and everything in between. Also, besides the actual methods used, there are the methods which performers *say* they use … but that's a whole different book! No matter which method you use, the escape is all about controlling and preserving slack in certain places of the jacket at certain times. It took me a year to feel confident enough to perform it on stage.

NOVEMBER 2010: I was fourteen, pitching the "Longest amount of time in a straitjacket" to Guinness World Records. I remember telling all my friends at school that something big was coming. I even sent out a bunch of tweets to foreshadow my success. Like, *"The ball is rolling!"* Tantalizing stuff. I could not wait. If I had a world record, I would be popular!

Naturally, there's a process to these things. First, you send Guinness an email with the name of the existing record you wish to break, how you're planning on breaking it, and how you'll prove this. Once you break the record, you send proof to Guinness for validation. This can take up to three years. And Guinness can reject you at any point in the process. A lot of work to be popular.

If you're setting a new record, the process is even more difficult. Setting a record means you're proposing a new challenge that no one has ever attempted. The proposal takes six weeks for review alone.

No magician had ever spent more than a night in a straitjacket before, at least not from what I found. Everybody thinks of the straitjacket as something to escape from. That's why this was different. What's the worst part of a breakup? When you're over it, or the time you spend sitting in the shit? It's the same with straitjackets. Uncomfortable and lonely. I wrote a proposal to Guinness. And I waited a month to hear back.

23.09.2010

A letter from Guinness World Records:

Dear Mr. Correia,

Thank you for sending us the details of your recent record attempt for 'Longest amount of time inside of a straitjacket'. We are afraid to say that we are unable to accept this as a Guinness World Record.

Unfortunately, with endurance records of this nature, we have a minimum age limit of sixteen years old. From then until age eighteen, a consent form must be signed by the claimant's parents/guardians. You are more than welcome to reapply once you are old enough.

Once again, thank you for your interest in Guinness World Records.

Well, I was going to be sixteen in two years and in that time, I could plan an even stronger stunt. No big deal.

I focused my energy elsewhere: a benefit performance for Parkinson's disease in honour of my hero, Michael J. Fox.

Michael has been my hero for as long as I can remember. When I was in grade four, I saw *Back to the Future* for the first time, and was completely enchanted. I wanted to buy a DeLorean and travel through time. But Michael was the best part. His performance seemed so honest. I made it my personal goal to watch every single one of his movies. My obsession with attention? It was nothing compared to my obsession with Michael J. Fox.

I remember the exact moment I found out he had Parkinson's disease.

Impossible. How could somebody so positive be affected by something so negative? If you were a good person, the world would protect you, right?[10] It didn't make any sense. I began telling myself they'd find a cure soon, and one day my hero would become healthy again. Eventually, I would help to make it happen. I did plenty of research on the disease and devoted all my school presentations to it.

Armed with years of public speaking experience, here is the disease explained in my own words: Parkinson's attacks the brain. The brain produces a chemical called dopamine, which is responsible for sending motor signals to the body. Parkinson's affects the development of this chemical, causing neurons to fire abnormally. This leads to tremors. Most people think of shaking when they think of Parkinson's, but the disease can also cause stiffness, slurred speech, difficulty with facial animation, and a slew of other symptoms.

While it typically affects one in one hundred people over the age of sixty, early onset Parkinson's can affect people as young as eighteen. People suffering from it deal with the slow deterioration of their motor skills. Everyday tasks become more and more difficult, until the brain's dopamine production ceases completely.

A benefit show for the disease had been on my radar since I was nine, but I didn't have a show I felt confident about until I'd met Scott. Planning a stunt was enough on its own, let alone an entire benefit event. And on top of all this, I was still in high school, and am told we were assigned homework too![11] Which led to other issues. How would I do my schoolwork in a straitjacket? Typing with a pencil in my teeth? Gym class? Hopefully we played a lot of soccer. Where would all the cameras go? Would I be popular or not? I would have to convince all my teachers, the principal, the superintendent, and so on. Maybe Guinness denying me was for the best.

---

10 I wish I had the naïveté of my nine-year-old self.

11 I never paid attention.

When I turned sixteen, my drama teacher asked if I wanted to audition for a new play by an up-and-coming Canadian playwright, Hannah Moscovitch. It was a quick *"no,"* since I would obviously be busy setting a world record, but she made me read the script. It was good. After two callbacks, I was cast as Israel in *The Children's Republic.* Since I was now in a professional theatre production, the stunt would have to wait, again. Which was okay, because the play featured Canadian actor Kelli Fox … who I later found out was the sister of Michael J. Fox. I never told Kelli I was a Michael fan, because I ended up just being a Kelli fan. She remains the sweetest actor I've ever worked with. She was exceptionally generous and helpful in the work.

When my untimely development of acute laryngitis led to the cancellation of a performance, Kelli went out and bought the ingredients for her miracle ginger drink and made it in my dressing room after everyone had left. I was up and running the next day. She was just that kind of person, always going out of her way for others. On closing night, I found a gift on my dressing room table. It was a book by her brother called *A Funny Thing Happened on the Way to the Future.* I opened it. There was a signature on the first page.

"Mark, Live out loud!

- Michael J. Fox"

How did she know?

That show convinced me to pursue acting after high school. I started researching post-secondary acting schools and narrowed my sights on the National Theatre School of Canada (NTS). My big stunt idea and benefit show fell by the wayside. Getting into this school was now my latest obsession.

Between researching schools, stunts, and completing my final year of high school, I met the love of my life. Or rather, re-met. She's going to play a pretty integral role in this story, so pay attention.

I was driving back from a particularly tough day at school in the Honda CR-V my mom let me borrow, and there she was, sitting almost exactly where I had left her five years ago on my front porch. Jasmine Harper.

Jasmine and I were childhood friends. Her house was down the street from my mom's, and the best climbing tree on the block was in her front yard. At family barbecues, we'd both sit at the kids' table and dare each other to eat sand. She was a year younger, which seems like a lifetime when you're twelve (or seventeen). But to tell you the truth, she always made my palms sweat. She was mature, didn't fall for any (of my) stupid lines, and never laughed at any (of my) stupid jokes. She was tough as nails, had a strong opinion about almost everything, and was the only kid on the block who could get the ball on the string into the cup (things like this mattered at the time).

Her family moved when I started high school. A full three-hour drive away. I'd be lying if I said I didn't tear up when she packed her last box. She was my best friend and confidant for so long. Nothing I write now could give you an idea of what she meant to me.

"Jasmine Harper! On my doorstep?" I would've sworn I was in a movie if I knew I wasn't. The sunlight illuminated her freckles and sunk deep into her jet-black hair. There she was. Older. Different, no doubt, but the same kid who'd laughed as I crashed my bike onto her front lawn. She barrelled toward me and gave me a big hug, then immediately withdrew, suddenly shy.

"How ya been?" she asked, almost in a whisper. It took me a moment too long to answer. What can I say? My palms were sweating.

"Fine! What brings you here?"

"I wanted to see if your dad was home."

Different, but the same. She was joking, of course. A brand of humour I'd really missed. She was staying in Toronto for an indefinite amount of time to research makeup schools in the city. Her family was planning on moving yet again that summer (a much more manageable thirty-minute drive) and so she'd decided to drop by.

"I didn't know you were into makeup?"

"I'm pretty enough that I don't need it, but let me know if you ever want some tips."

When an hour that felt more like five minutes shot by, I realized I was crushing hard. So, riding on that warm fuzzy feeling, I asked her out. Just like that, I had my best friend back—and this time she didn't make me eat sand, which was a huge plus. We had spent some of our formative years together, and she's played a huge role in shaping the person I am today. (I'd also appreciate it if someone could tell me when my formative years are officially over.) Eventually, I graduated high school (score), and auditioned for the National Theatre School of Canada, which required reference letters from professionals in the field. I emailed my *Children's Republic* director, and she responded:

01.20.13

Hi Mark,

Well, good news and bad news.

As it turns out, I'm the new artistic director of the National Theatre School. So, while you can't use me as a reference, I do know your work already!

Even better. After the callback, I was accepted into NTS as one of only twelve students in my year. It was time to prepare for a new life in Montreal.

SOMETIME IN LATE 2013 *(NTS classroom):* Pacing the floor between classes, an inexplicable wave of inspiration rushes over me: I'm looking at my phone, and I see that Penn of Penn & Teller[12] is raising funds for an upcoming movie.

His campaign was on a crowdfunding website, and it was the first time I had seen something like that. I began a mock draft of what my own crowdfunding page would look like. Seemed like a quick way to make money.[13] I drafted a quick Parkinson's benefit idea to see how it would look. That's when my idea reached a level of clarity it hadn't before.

The straitjacket was a great metaphor for the constrictive nature of Parkinson's disease. Why plan a benefit show when I could use my stunt as the benefit? And why had it taken me so long to come up with this? And was I going to be late for my next class?[14]

---

12 My favourite magical duo.

13 Maybe my naïveté was well and intact.

14 Yes, I was.

WALKING THE WALK

(Personal Hell: My apartment in Montreal where I planned the stunt—2013)

This is the beginning. Not like the beginning-beginning, but the beginning of the journey. The beginning of Escaping Parkinson's. I'd done three years of dreaming. Now it was time to get my hands dirty.[15]

I decided to execute my stunt in July 2014, meaning I had eight months to prepare. My good friend Rosemary Reid was the first person I brought on board. Along with being a talented magician, she was a talented creative writer. Here's what a rough outline of the stunt looked like:

- A daily video blog, attempting hilarious everyday tasks.
- If someone donated one hundred dollars, their name would be written on the jacket.
- If a corporate sponsor donated one thousand dollars, the company name would be written on the jacket.
- I'd reapply for a Guinness World Record.
- I'd obtain a quote from Michael J. Fox.

If we could solidify this, we'd have something special on our dirty hands.

The first step was research. I looked into the longest amount of time anyone had spent in the restraint. There were no recorded accounts for the longest time in a straitjacket. Even in 1920s prison facilities, people would be unbuckled for breaks or showers. My personal best was about four hours. So that wasn't exactly great. I tried sleeping in it and had night terrors. Not very promising. When I told Scott about my crazy plan, he immediately wired me some money to get things moving. I hope all of you have a Scott in your life.

A small town[16] outside of Montreal was my home due to my broke student status. I was living in a room at my aunt's house to save money. My school was a forty-five-minute train ride away. I would get home,

---

15 This is going to become very funny later in the book.

16 Again, big town.

work well into the night, get my thoughts down on paper, and make some phone calls.

Once my research was compiled, I sent an application to Guinness, again. It turned out that for records like "World's longest roller coaster ride," bathroom breaks were permitted. Essentially, I could take off the jacket for breaks. Obviously, this would help with my physical concerns, but I didn't like the idea of taking the jacket off. You can't take off Parkinson's. If I really wanted to be an ally to this community, I would have to push myself. I would have to find a way to pee without using my hands. That's me: centre of attention, and stubborn.

Why fourteen days? I hear you, reader. For one, it had to be long enough to scare off other magicians. (Those assholes are crazy. Didn't you read Scott's greatest hits list?) Second, I was fourteen when I planned the stunt. Third, it was 2014 (looking back, I should have done 2,014 days, but hindsight is 2020).

As I waited to hear back from Guinness, I sent the first outline to some very influential magicians I had met attending a magic camp called Sorcerers Safari, and I promise it was exactly what you're picturing (it has since closed down).

I was overwhelmed in the beginning, so I'd summarize my ideas and write them, saying: *"Hey, is there any way you can help me at all?"* which should have been followed by: *"… because I have no idea what the hell I'm doing!"*

Other than influential magicians I had camped with, there were the people in my personal life I needed help from. Like my girlfriend! Jasmine and I were taking an immediate plunge into a long-distance relationship. She was in Toronto, and I was five and a half hours away in Montreal. We'd make the train ride when we could, but spent most of our time on the phone. When I pitched her the stunt idea, she seemed skeptical. I told her Kelli (from *The Children's Republic*, for those of you who are not committing every detail of my life to memory) could help me get in contact with Mr. Fox, and maybe I'd even meet him! And then I'd be on The Ellen DeGeneres Show! There's reason to be skeptical when your boyfriend is talking about meeting Ellen DeGeneres and Michael J. Fox in the same sentence.

Jasmine was excited for me, but also probably didn't want to let me down. After all, I was hanging out in a room in my aunt's house, justifying living in a straitjacket for two weeks. She told me she would help, but that I should probably take things slower. Not something you ever want to hear from your long-distance girlfriend. I hadn't considered that these moments of discouragement would feel so personal.

Money was also an issue. Mostly, how to get it. We weren't super close, but I knew this commerce student, Jason D'Souza, whom I'd met through a mutual friend. Maybe he had sponsorship and budgeting insight that I didn't. Jason jumped at the opportunity to help and immediately said he was on board. He had drive, passion, and a sense of humour that would no doubt come in handy, but he also didn't quite understand how sponsorships could work. I was getting ahead of myself.

People were doubting me, and it was not their fault. But it was enough to make me doubt myself. I knew everything would go according to plan, but the truth is, you can never really *know*. So, whether it was sheer determination to prove them wrong, dumb luck, or a gut feeling I couldn't deny, I plodded forward with my big idea one step at a time. What's the worst that could happen?[17]

8.10.13

An email from Guinness World Records:

Claim ID: 443837

Dear Mr. Correia,

Thank you for sending us the details of your proposed record

---

17 If you say this, something bad is about to happen.

attempt for 'Longest amount of time in a straitjacket.'

Unfortunately, after thoroughly reviewing your application with members of our research team, we are afraid to say that we're unable to accept your proposal as a Guinness World Records title.

Our team of expert record managers receive thousands of new record proposals every year from all over the world, which are carefully assessed to establish if they meet our stringent criteria. Every record verified by Guinness World Records must be measurable by a single superlative, verifiable, standardizable, breakable, and also be able to present an element of skill.

Only a handful of new records categories are accepted every year.

Whilst we fully appreciate this is not the decision you were hoping for, we trust that you will understand our position.

Once again, thank you for contacting Guinness World Records.

Kind regards,

Records Management Team

Six weeks to find out I wouldn't be the most popular kid in school. Now what? Call off the stunt entirely, or focus all my energy on the Michael J. Fox Foundation?

The choice was obvious. This was a blessing in disguise. Now I could take my stunt in any direction I wanted. So, why did it feel like such a huge failure?

After texting Scott the bad news, he let me in on a secret. There are two world record organizations: Guinness and RecordSetter. RecordSetter is a company that takes in new records and immediately chooses to accept or reject them. There's no six-week waiting process, and there are fewer rules about what makes an "appropriate record." Want to set a record for "Most pies in the face in one minute"? Why not! This was the sort of attitude I wanted on my side. However, if the Michael J. Fox Foundation wasn't on board, there was no point in doing any of this. I put RecordSetter aside and looked into Team Fox, the grassroots community of the foundation.

If you're a Team Fox fundraiser, you have access to all the foundation's logos, names, and a personalized fundraising webpage. In other words, we wouldn't have to use a crowdsourcing site. After securing my spot on the Team Fox roster, I was assigned a representative: Liz.

I still ran a crowdsourcing campaign to fundraise the overhead costs of the project. My family and friends came together to support my little idea. Total donations from those friends and family (including extended relatives) totalled a whopping $297.35! Cue the anxiety about whether this would raise *any* money for the Michael J. Fox Foundation.

Now I had a small team, no fundraising dollars (no dollars whatsoever), lots of ideas, but no direction. I needed a win, but a win wasn't coming just yet. In class, I would dream up slogans, websites, photos. I would sit alone in the cafeteria on my lunch break writing proposals. Great, another obsession. It was up to me to stay motivated and to motivate the people around me.

The cause kept me going. Parkinson's sucks. A lot of the tremor symptoms can be credited to other diseases as well, so it's hard to determine if you even have the disease. By the time tremors are present, it has already progressed significantly.

I learned that the bobbing, swaying, and rocking that comes with Parkinson's is not actually a symptom of the disease. These movements are side effects from the medication, Levodopa (the same drug they've been using since 1960). Its purpose is to deliver more dopamine to the brain, in order to simulate normal function. The drug actually eradicates many symptoms of Parkinson's, but the side effects can be far worse. It can take a long time to find an effective dosage. I first met someone with the disease in the fifth grade while doing one of my many Parkinson's related school projects. My teacher arranged for me to meet with her husband who suffered from the illness. His wife understood him perfectly, but I had to focus intently on his mouth to make out each word. He showed me how he signed his name, holding his wrist with his other hand to steady the tremors. At one point, I asked what the most annoying part of the disease was. He said, *"Always having to repeat myself."* I remember thinking that I was boring him with my questions. But he later explained that his face was locked into one expression most of the time, and that although he could change it, it took significant effort to show emotion. I'm sure you can imagine what this meant for an aspiring actor.

Upon watching a Parkinson's patient navigate these symptoms, it quickly became clear how debilitating the disease could be. Many patients face these obstacles each day and turn their experiences into something positive. They take a life-changing circumstance and use it to do just that: Change their lives. So, what was stopping me from changing mine?

The magicians began answering my emails. Wayne Houchin (magician and stuntman), took the time to send over some pointers:

10.28.13

Hi Mark!

Be as prepared as possible. If you're planning on spending a week in the jacket, you should do that (privately) prior to doing the stunt publicly. I know that may sound extreme, but the ideal situation is this:

You know for a fact that you can accomplish the stunt without causing any harm to yourself. You have already discovered the unexpected problems, allowing you to plan for them during the (public) stunt.

This allows you to really focus on the performance, promotion, and marketing during the actual stunt, instead of also dealing with unexpected problems.

- Wayne

PS: Even if you don't want to commit to (privately) testing the stunt for the full week, just commit to doing it for 3 or 4 days. You really want to give yourself time to test how it will feel to sleep, go to the bathroom, deal with muscle cramps, etc.

He also agreed to tweet while I was in the jacket to notify his fans. Aaron Fisher agreed to tweet as well.[18]

11.23.13

Hey Mark,

Let me know when it's time and I'll be happy to put you out on my media networks! Best of luck on this, man. I hear you're kicking ass wherever you go!

- Aaron

11.14.13

Hey! Same camera person/editor is KEY! You need a passionate high school or college student. It'll cost you, but you won't have to buy a camera and the stress it'll save you is key. Get your pits cleaned.

- Eric Leclerc

Lee Asher chose to call me. That phone call really shaped how I viewed the presentation of the stunt. He had a ton of advice for me. An over-whelming amount, in fact. He also told me that I shouldn't draw any direct parallels between Parkinson's and a straitjacket. They're not even

---

18 Twitter was still a thing that people did.

close to the same thing. He was right. We rejigged all our text, being careful not to patronize. But he had a better idea.

A video. The best way to explain the stunt would be on camera. Duh. Only now I needed a script and a film team. The only time I had off from school was the Christmas break; I considered it a gift to myself. I asked my friend and fellow Kool Kat, Sanjay Parker, to be the shoot manager, and he quickly agreed. Sanjay was our group's leader, herding us like a circus ring master. Wildly unusual, but undeniably organized.

I had a lot on my plate, but it wasn't like I was studying astrophysics. This was, after all, a glorified magic trick … right?

I wrote the script, sent letters to Ellen, and sent a lot of pitches to different corporations. I was working away, but somehow the workload was only growing. If I thought I felt alone before, the answers from the corporations would enforce that tenfold.

My phone would buzz at school, my heart would flutter, and then I would read: *"We're sorry Mr. Correia, at this moment in time our corporation does not have the funds to support your fundraiser, we wish you the best of luck and hope you continue to buy (insert product name) in the future!"*

At this point, my relationship with Jasmine was suffering. A long-distance relationship suffering? Unusual. I just never felt like talking about anything but the stunt.[19] I told her I was under a lot of stress.
"How are you stressed," she said. *"All you're doing is answering emails?"*

Fair. I was in love, I had my family, I was with my friends, but the fact was I had something to prove to myself. I think I had to prove to myself that I wasn't lazy … something I heard from my teachers and parents a lot as a kid. Somewhere along the line, completing the stunt became a reflection of me. If I failed, if I stopped, then I'd have to admit to the world that

---

19 It would be a while before I found out my need to be the centre of attention was costing me relationships.

maybe I wasn't as special as I had led everyone to believe. I'm pretty sure the name for that is imposter syndrome.

My mom kept saying that I was flying by the seat of my pants. *"Do you even know what you're doing with this whole thing, or are you just winging it?"*

That hurt. My dad wanted me to do it his way, always checking up on my progress and offering what I deemed to be "stupid suggestions." I knew they meant well, so I kept blaming myself. Never taking any time to relax. I was chasing a feeling of satisfaction that wouldn't come unless I took the time to appreciate what I'd done so far.

I was getting rejected by multibillion-dollar corporations every day, so it was time to contact Kelli about her brother. Another rejection couldn't hurt, right?

11.18.13

Oh Mark, you make me weep.

I'm going to do whatever I can to make sure your effort gets Michael's attention. I don't know what I would suggest to improve what you've offered. My plate is a little full at the moment so just give me a bit of time, but I'll do what I can for you. Keep doing everything else you're doing too.

- Kelli

That's Kelli. She sent an email to Michael's team and forwarded the message to me:

12.4.13

Hi,

I'm writing to give you a heads up that you can expect to hear from a young friend of mine. He's a kid named Mark that I worked with a couple of years ago when he was still in high school. He's a pretty special guy and, along with being a terrific young actor, is a truly talented magician. He specializes in escapes! Who knew anyone really did that anymore?

Anyway, he's terrific and he has a pretty grand plan for a fundraiser. It's a straitjacket stunt on live TV and he wants to use it to raise funds for the foundation. He's after corporate sponsorship and some high-profile support for this stunt in the hopes of maximizing the fundraising effort. He would give anything to have Michael acknowledge his effort. He's kind of a superfan and has taken this on to honour the inspiration Michael has been to him in his career.

Thanks for this.

When I heard the response, my jaw dropped. His team agreed to help with some tweets from Michael, by sending anything I might need over to Toronto, and by setting me up with the Team Fox offices in New York City! Suddenly, I didn't give one fuck about multizillion-dollar businesses. Michael J. Fox said yes ... to me! I began communicating with Michael's team and was, therefore, one step closer to my hero. They expressed their commitment to the project in one correspondence, saying: *"We will do whatever we can to help."*

"Whatever we can to help"? I couldn't believe my eyes. It was surreal. In the midst of all this supposed failure, I got my win. I came on strong and asked if Michael would be willing to film a video clip offering his support. I bugged his team every day. It was like getting my first phone number.

Unfortunately, Michael was working on a new TV show and his schedule didn't allow him to film the clip, but he took the time to send over this amazing quote:

> *"Team Fox members have always brought a certain amount of magic to their events, but Escaping Parkinson's takes it to another level. Our Foundation is grateful for Mark Correia's creativity and sheer lunacy in helping bring us one step closer to a cure."*

> *– Michael J. Fox.*

With this boost of confidence, I finished my script and started assembling my own team. I contacted a filmmaker from high school and asked if he'd shoot the promo video for nothing. He jumped on the idea and told me that he would put together a team of cinematographers and editors and then get back to me. Sanjay's job was to keep us all on track. I have trouble with time management because it's just so fun getting distracted.[20]

A new video meant I needed a new website. So, I reached out to my web designer (who happened to be the mother of Katie Cohen, my fellow actor in *The Children's Republic*. I had chatted with Katie about our love for Michael J. Fox a couple of times on her kitchen floor while eating her mom's leftover pancakes—but I digress), and she agreed to do it, also for nothing.

MID-2013 *(Montreal):* Meanwhile, one friend was keeping me sane. Erik Berg is an artist, a poet, and my best friend from NTS. He kept my brain healthy. I'll be careful not to oversell him here because he wouldn't like that, but he's a genius.

I couldn't get a read on Erik when we first met. He seemed committed to art, but a bit in his own world. On the way to a welcome party one night, we stopped outside the house and talked. He had to run home and FaceTime with his girlfriend who lived in his hometown of Winnipeg. That was something I could identify with. *"I love a girl in a faraway place too."*

Soon, I was spending nights at Erik's apartment in Montreal's Plateau neighbourhood to avoid the subway ride to my aunt's. He slept on the floor the first night, but we got comfortable quickly and eventually slept in the same bed. Since I was broke, he would cook meals for me as I worked on the stunt on his kitchen floor. It was great. I have to admit, I liked the apartment and I liked chatting with Erik even more. Things progressed.

---

20 I hope you are having a fun time reading this in 2055.

Erik and I fell in love, put a lease on a cottage, and we've recently adopted. I gave up on the stunt and settled down with him in the country.[21]

But seriously, we did become very close, very quickly. Having gotten used to how convenient it was to stay at Erik's, the trek to my aunt's place became unbearable, and in December I moved into the apartment down the hall from him. My mom agreed to cover the difference in rent, and it was settled.

Jasmine and I Skyped often.[22] I'd fold laundry while she taught me all about colour theory, and on Tuesdays we'd order the same takeout, pretending to eat together. We tried to follow that rule about not going to bed angry, but some nights we'd be up until two in the morning, fighting. It's hard to admit, but the stunt hurt us. Actually, maybe it's harder to admit that it wasn't just the stunt.

School was out for the holidays. I took the train home in secret. My first plan of action had nothing to do with straitjackets. This time, I was the one waiting on the front step when Jasmine turned into the driveway of the house she was staying at in Toronto. This was a lot less romantic than it seems, as it was December in Canada and I, as usual, underestimated the weather and her time in traffic. She cupped her hands around my red ears and told me how utterly stupid I was for not waiting in the car. Maybe it was a little romantic. I suggested she learn from my mistake and bundle up nicely, because I had a date planned.

Jasmine took guesses at our destination the entire ride to it (and generated some much better ideas in the process), only to uncover the truth in the last five minutes. When we arrived at the beaten-up basketball net

---

21 If you've skipped to the last page and broken my trust, you'll recognize my tongue-in-cheek approach to writing.

22 This was before the entire world collectively switched to Zoom.

behind her old house in Oakville, I popped the trunk and revealed the tattered ball we'd played with as children. Cute as hell. I know.

We giggled and screamed and practiced dunking on one another. There was a lot more sexual tension now than there was at twelve. Our faces burned from the cold, but damn, it felt good to be home.

We made a point of seeing each other every day while I was back. Even just for a moment. Suddenly, we weren't fighting anymore. Who knew that seeing each other would be such a pressure reliever?

It instilled me with hope: the problem wasn't us, it was the distance between us. I knew that now.

Work picked up again. Me, Sanjay, and the crew loaded the gear into my mom's car and drove around Toronto shooting my bound antics in interesting locations. On the street, in a grocery store, and while trying on shoes. The reactions were the most interesting. I was new to this. For the most part, people didn't acknowledge me at all. They didn't stare, they didn't even look, they just acted like I didn't exist.

The next morning, we arrived at our film studio. Jasmine did my hair and makeup and took photos with my phone for Instagram. I was having trouble memorizing my lines. I'm an actor, but I can't play myself. There were some friendly arguments over what sounded more natural. I guess people were passionate. This was all good. Then it was time for the money shot. The bathroom. I had everyone in stitches as I tried to use a urinal. We chose it as the video's opening hook. It'd only been an hour, but my knuckles were bright red where the jacket had been rubbing against them. I needed a new position for my hands. We broke for lunch after, and I paid for the food. It was the least I could do.

We had all the footage we needed for our promo video. Now it was up to the director to work his editing magic. We needed a rough cut by February and a finished product by the end of March.

I was free to enjoy Christmas with my family. We made gingerbread houses and did all that cute holiday garbage. On Christmas morning, I found a gift from Jas on the porch. Tap shoes … because I loved *Singin' in the Rain* as a kid.[23] I always get this empty feeling on Christmas. There's this expectation of joy with limited time to achieve it. It feels like it's over before it even begins. And then it was. My time in Toronto was up. Jasmine took me to the train. As beautiful as our time together was, I think we both knew we were heading back into murky waters. We promised to try our best, to be kind and thoughtful, and never forget how happy we made each other. And just like that, I was back in Montreal.

JANUARY 2014: Six months until the stunt. I sent photos to my graphic designer, and she sent me business card designs. I could leave these at hipster-vegan restaurants around the condiment section so people could ignore them. The front of the card featured photos of me in the jacket and thick white text that read:

"ESCAPING PARKINSON'S:
1 STRAITJACKET. 2 WEEKS. 4 PARKINSON'S."

I needed a publicity team. A good publicity team can cost thousands, but it's totally worth it. Have you ever tried to contact the media yourself? Here's some advice: Don't.

I pitched the stunt to my friend's mother, who ran a PR firm called Idea Workshop. I waited nervously for three days before hearing that she wanted to represent me. I was assigned Marion as my publicist, and she put together a press release. Big win.

---

23 The movie, not the activity.

That was more money I didn't have, though. I called my uncle John (the owner of some McDonald's restaurants in Ottawa) and asked if his company would be willing to sponsor the stunt. He told me he'd be in Montreal soon and wanted to meet.

He arrived with my aunt Rachel and they took me out for dinner. I hadn't eaten a proper meal in weeks. John said he would cover all my PR costs and with that, I had my first official corporate sponsor; their name was promptly added to the jacket. It came just in time. I was funnelling more and more grocery money into Escaping Parkinson's. Dinner would've been enough.

My project was coming together, but now my relationship was falling apart. I was getting tired of the juggling act.[24] The strain on our relationship returned almost immediately. It just felt like if I wasn't physically present, I couldn't be present at all. Jasmine and I fought on the night I returned. This time I couldn't handle letting it go. There was a problem, and we were going to talk it through until we solved it because we loved each other and that was the only thing that mattered. I made her stay up until four in the morning to finish it. She was so exhausted she could barely talk, but she stayed. For me. Do I remember what we fought about for five hours? Of course not. Nothing improved over the next couple of days.

SOMETIME IN EARLY 2014: Jasmine called me … and broke up with me.

Everything screeched to a halt. I panicked. I told her I had to see her. I told her I was sorry. I told her a lot, but none of it mattered. She hung up. She was done. Worst of all, she was right.

---

24 The metaphor, not the activity.

I broke down in Erik's apartment. It didn't feel real. It couldn't be. I still loved her. She still loved me. I mean she must, even just a little. Right?

I called the school and told them I was dropping out and catching the next train to Toronto. Dramatic? It didn't feel dramatic at the time. The artistic director told me to come to her office. She convinced me to stay for another week. Nothing was the same after that. I'd lost my best friend. I tried contacting her all day, to no avail. It wasn't her fault though. I was in love with mys— stunt … more than anything else.

Somehow, I convinced Jasmine to come visit one last time, for a proper goodbye. We kissed as soon as she got off the bus and spent the whole weekend making everything more confusing. Before she left, she told me she had a lot of hope, but needed time. We were still broken up, but we were in love, and once more, we were apart.

I distracted myself by sending emails and tweaking the promo video. I was just killing time until I could see Jasmine in person again.

After she left, she started calling. We'd write and revise the rules of what we were to each other. But this back-and-forth wasn't helping either of us feel any more stable. Jasmine finally gave me the closure I needed: *"I shouldn't have told you to wait. I don't want to talk until you're back in the summer. Focus on you. I'll focus on me."*

No phone calls, no texts, no nothing, for months. An endurance stunt I hadn't accounted for.

I sat in the corner of my apartment with the lights off. How could I just forget about her? Was it really that easy for her to forget about me? I grabbed my shirt and tore through it. The buttons popped off and rolled all over the apartment. Scattering under the furniture like the German cockroaches I shared board with. I was hurt and angry and alone. As opposed to renouncing this type of drama, I leaned into it. Sounds crazy now, sure, but I was hurting and it helped. Did my obsessions lead to this, or was it something else entirely?

March was ending, and I had managed to finish my work. Everything was ready to launch. Jason picked up where Jasmine had left off and was starting to become a close friend as well. The plan was to release what we'd been planning in mid-April. The only thing missing was music for the video. Erik's old roommate was a composer, and agreed to create something.

APRIL 2014: Promo Video Release day. *"This July 7–21, I'm going to spend two weeks in a straitjacket. For Parkinson's disease research."* Suddenly, this little idea was a big deal. My phone was vibrating off the hook. (Can something vibrate off the hook?) By the time I got home from school, the video had climbed to ten thousand views and a hundred people had shared it on Facebook. My inbox was full of people wanting to help. People I barely knew were clamouring for more information. At the end of the day, my link had five hundred shares, twenty thousand views, and everyone was offering to pull in favours. How surreal. Wasn't I just worrying non-stop twelve hours earlier?

4.12.14

Hi Mark,

Thank you so much for doing this to bring attention to Parkinson's. It is such an insidious disease. My mother has had it for many years and lives with me.

Keep up the inspiring work,

Anonymous

4.21.14

Your video is awesome and I love the idea. My granddad died of Parkinson's so it's close to my heart also. Will definitely be donating. Well done.

Anonymous

4.24.14

I saw your video and I'd just like to say thank you. Parkinson's has really affected my family; Parkinson's disease killed my grandfather and great grandmother. I think what you're doing is amazing and creative and it really means a lot to me and so many others, so thank you. I really hope you are able to spread this great cause.

Anonymous

Escaping Parkinson's became a big conversation point while out to dinner with some friends the next day. Consider me a rude guest who couldn't stop checking his phone all night. My Twitter followers had climbed to 6,500 (again, this was a big deal at the time). Friends I hadn't spoken to in years were messaging me just to say *"Hey"* (what a coincidence). People seemed to be taking an interest. Selfishly, the notification that caught my eye was a missed call from Jasmine Harper.

The stunt was in a good place, so I took Easter weekend off and brought Erik with me to Oakville. I needed to find time to be a kid and shut off from the project for a while.

Jasmine had texted, asking if I had any free time, but I promised myself I wouldn't see her. A simple: *"I don't think I can, all the best,"* was the right move. I was starting to resent how she had handled the breakup, which I don't think is an uncommon occurrence (though potentially not a mature reaction).

On Saturday, Erik and I took my mom's car and drove to ESA (my former high school) in the middle of the night. We walked around the school's perimeter, looking into windows. I showed him where my locker was, a few of my classrooms, and where I'd made certain memories. We then got back in the car and drove home. I did hear a less-than-legal story that occurred that same night, though. A friend of mine, let's call him David, has this crazy story about breaking into the school! I remember it in detail. Here goes:

So, David was standing with (let's call him) Jack by his side. He asked Jack if he wanted to try and climb onto the roof. Of course he did. They jumped onto a dumpster and scaled the wall onto the building.

They looked out over the field, everything calm and still from up there. David had been on the school roof once before, executing a prank with some classmates, so he showed Jack around. They walked over to this huge chimney, twenty or thirty feet tall with a metal rung ladder, and started climbing. You could see the entire city from the top. Every rooftop, every glimmering light. But they had nowhere to stand because of the two giant holes leading straight into the school. It was a chimney, after all. The only thing holding them was the will of their fingers. It was a cold night and the metal rungs stung their hands, so they didn't stay up there long.

They sauntered over to some windows and looked inside the upstairs classrooms. David pushed on one. *"How funny would it be if this op—"*

The window swung open. *Oh no*, he thought.

"What now?" said Jack, grinning.

They could see a stairwell under the window, about an eight-foot drop. David was pretty sure the school had motion detectors, so he reached inside and waved his arm up and down. Nothing.

"If the alarm goes off, we probably have, what? Five minutes to get out of here?" Ambulances are fast, sure, but theft is a big deal! Jack went in first. David held his bag as Jack squeezed into the school and did a little

wiggling to get his ass through. He lowered himself down and released his grip.

"Move around. Make sure there are no alarms," suggested David. Jack jumped, waved his arms, made some noise. Nothing. David threw his own stuff down, taking out his wallet, phone, and car keys and stuffing them into his coat pocket before slipping it through to Jack. He went in headfirst, planning to swing his legs around him after. The top half of his body slid through with ease before getting stuck at his waist.

Then: *WOOH-WOOH-WOOH-WOOH.* Alarms. Wailing. Not a siren, not beeping, *wailing.* Non-stop wailing. *WOOH-WOOH-WOOH-WOOH.*

David and Jack locked eyes. Horrified. David started pulling himself back out, scratching his hips on the sides of the window.

"Hurry! Five minutes!" He screamed.

WOOH-WOOH-WOOH-WOOH.

Jack ran to the window and threw David's coat back up, missing. He cocked back and threw it again. David caught it. Then he grabbed Jack's arm and started pulling him up and through. It was too high. He looked across the field. He could feel the school shaking beneath his feet. The sound of the alarm blaring across the neighbourhood.

WOOH-WOOH-WOOH-WOOH.

Jack jumped up and caught the edge of the window, clambering out. At this point, David was already hanging off the roof. A fifteen-foot drop at least. Jack looked over at him.

"No! You're not going—" David let go. He hit the grass. A ringing sound blared in his ear. He rolled over his shoulder and stood up, disoriented but uninjured.

"GO! GO!" Jack threw his stuff down and leapt. He hit the ground. Hard. His knee connected with his chin. It split open. Blood dripped down his neck.

"Fuck! Are you—" he was already running toward David.

They could still hear the alarm from across the parking lot. David put his hand in his pocket, desperately searching for his keys.

"Where are my keys?" he cried. *"Throw me my coat!"*

He quickly found the keys, shoved them into the ignition, and cranked into reverse before Jack was even inside. Then he floored it, skidding and sending Jack flying back into his seat. The smell of burnt rubber. His heart raced. The sound of police sirens now very clear in the distance.

They laughed as they tore down the highway. Safe. Though Jack's glasses were gone. He'd probably lost them in the fall. They counted their victories and drove off into the night.

Wild story, huh? The drama! Legend has it, David and Jack returned the next day and actually found Eri— I mean, Jack's glasses in the grass … I wish I'd been there to see it.

MAY 3, 2014: School is officially out for summer. Two months left before the stunt. one thousand dollars raised so far. Not bad. Not great.

My search for a daily video editor began. They had to be willing to receive footage every day for two weeks, sift through it overnight, and cut it into something entertaining the next day. *"Oh, and you want me to work for free? Sign me up!"*

My friend Max messaged me; he had more film experience than any of us, and expressed an interest in stepping on board. On board he came.

My first stop upon arriving in the city should have been stunt related, but instead I drove to Jasmine's house on a whim (because that's what you do when you're stupid and in love). Except now we were in a messy sort of love. The time had helped. We spoke all night, doing our best to convince each other we were different people.[25] She asked if she could still be part of the stunt and I (secretly hoping she would) said yes.

---

25 We weren't.

Jason and I were becoming close friends, cracking down on the remaining work together. With his advice, we'd paid for spots on popular blogs and online advertisements. Our lack of confirmed media interest was a huge bummer. My goal was fifteen thousand dollars and we had only raised one thousand. I'm not great at math, but I know those numbers aren't close. We would need more attention if we wanted more money.

Hand billing started. First at the train station, during the morning rush. Me, Jasmine, and Jason made our way to the station. They strapped me into the jacket and we began selling our story.

"Don't take no for an answer. Put this card in their hands," I instructed. Jasmine shoved the cards in people's faces while Jason took the time to explain the cause. Neither approach worked.

A quick rundown of the day: *"Hi, would you like to help end Parkinson's disease?"*

"No."

Not too comforting. We tried different tactics.

"My friend is wearing a straitjacket for Michael J. Fox." What? *"We're setting a world record!"* You are?

At one point I began yelling, *"You might win ten thousand dollars!"* I wasn't lying. People might win ten thousand dollars—of course they might. It happens occasionally. The postcard wouldn't lead to it directly, but they might win the money elsewhere. Logistics.

One person asked: *"How long do I have to wear it?"* Jason tried to explain that they wouldn't be wearing the jacket at all, but I don't think they ever understood. A lot of people asked how I would use the bathroom. I'd smile and say, *"Not easily."*

We thought we might make a bigger impact somewhere … bigger. How about Toronto's largest shopping centre? We showed up to the Eaton Centre with a briefcase full of postcards, found a central spot, and opened the case. I put on the jacket. People seemed more interested. As they started asking more questions, security arrived.

"This wasn't cleared with us."

Raising money for charity while security guards bark about private property can be frustrating.

"I'm just going to give out the rest of my print." I continued placing cards into open hands. My team looked worried. The security guard followed me.

"Sir, you need to stop."

I didn't care, I kept going.

Another security guard came to help, so I ran up the escalator, handing out print along the way. They caught me eventually and gave me strict instructions to leave the mall. We did.

We needed more awareness, so I started booking more shows (it's that easy). I contacted a friend of mine, Scott Graham. He's an author, motivational speaker, and summer camp organizer, and he helped put me in front of more audiences. Accompanying him to events meant an opportunity to plug the stunt. This is how the rest of the month went. Moving around different cities, spreading the word.

A woman sent me an email about some concerts she'd organized. She also suffered from a degenerative disease and wanted to help. After sending along a list of cities she was planning shows in, she offered me an opportunity to promote the project at them. This was the exposure I was looking for!

The first event was in Guelph. I asked Jason if he would accompany me. His mom drove us. We passed many beautiful venues before pulling into *our* venue. We didn't totally fit in at a punk show or dive bar. The organizer welcomed us graciously and showed me to my booth … in the back behind the coat check. There were only twenty people there and Jason was one of them. I took the mic at one point, spouted some gibberish about

Michael J. Fox, and went back to my table. Some people had dropped a few coins into our bucket, and we made an impressive $2.50.

I felt so defeated that I thanked the organizer for everything and cancelled my appearance at the Toronto event.[26]

The last spot on my self-proclaimed press tour was a middle school outside of Toronto.[27] Jasmine accompanied me this time. I gave a speech about following your dreams and did not sugar-coat my thoughts on the education system. Then I did a few tricks, told them about myself, and plugged the stunt. Every rotation of kids had competing class clowns, so I was more at home than at the punk concert.

I reminded them that faculty often forgot how much pressure they put on students, and that school wasn't for everyone (it isn't). I told them I skipped plenty of class to focus on more important things. That got their attention. Especially the teacher's. I revealed that "keeping your options open" was a ridiculous notion, and how motivation increased when you said: *"Fuck back-up plans."* I think that's when the teacher made me wrap up early.

This project was already a roller coaster of emotions.

We were weeks away with no confirmed media spots, now resting at $1,500, when an old friend called to turn it around.

"Casey! How are you?" I said, pleasantly surprised.

"Hi Mark! I know you're looking for donations for your project, so I ran it past my dad, and he's agreed to donate ten percent of your goal!" I almost dropped the phone—$2,500—this is a huge number to an eighteen-year-old.

"He really loves what you're doing and wants to support any way he can. He's going to transfer the money soon."

---

26 Over two thousand people attended the Toronto event. Fuck.

27 Every town that isn't Toronto is outside of it.

This was by far the best news I'd heard. It was my second pivotal moment. People believed in this enough to give me $2,500? Just because the money didn't pour in at the beginning, didn't mean it wouldn't continue to trickle in throughout the process. It may seem obvious now, but that call helped me realize how numbers work. I thanked Casey profusely and hung up.

I answered as many emails as I could, but I was getting quite a few now!

6.20.14

Dear Mark!

I think your straitjacket thing is cool. So cool! A friend of mine collects them and he has hundreds. Keep up the good work.

-Erin

6.22.14

Hi Mark!

Thank you so much for writing back!

I love straitjackets and I just think it's so cool how you're using yours. Also, I love your videos on YouTube and the funny things you do in your SJ! I just really wanted to reach out and see if you would offer your perspective or experiences with them. Most people wear baggy straitjackets and you went with a red one, which I think is small. Wow, cool. I would wear a small too, I think. I still need to buy a real Posey. I had a black leather one but it's gone now. Sad. Anyways, it is so cool you wrote me back!

How is life going?

Your fan,

Mike

A black leather straitjacket? To each their own.[28]

They say that good things happen all at once. Actually, I don't know if they say that, but it's what happened next, so I'm saying it. In forty-eight hours, I had three media outlets on board (finally). Global's *The Morning Show* wanted me on the second day of the stunt. The *Oakville Beaver* (local newspaper) agreed on a front-page spread, and a popular radio show offered me airtime sometime in the middle. Now I had some traction, four thousand in fundraising dollars, and zero time left.

---

28 I prefer latex.

BUCKLE UP

© Personal Collection

(A Chat with Jason: Promoting Escaping Parkinson's at the mall—2014)

JUNE 10, 2014: Training time. The jacket took its toll in less than two hours. Complete with muscle spasms, aching, throbbing … but wait, there's more! Jasmine came over to help me figure out the bathroom. Also fun. I found a way to pee on my own. It wasn't pretty, and there was always a bit of … residue. Nothing to lose my head over. I was relieved when the number one goal was figured out. Now it was onto the number two goal. That didn't go so well. After much negotiating with the crotch strap, I developed a solid method. It was probably the most impressive task I'd completed thus far, but I don't want to reveal the method. (I'm a magician, dammit!) Since we've grown so close, I'll give you a hint: it involves shimmying a small vacuum up my pant leg … and the rest is self-explanatory. There, now you can focus on wondering how I got off.

Jasmine stayed over while I slept. We went to the coldest room in the house, the basement, and threw a mattress on the floor. It was June and I was in a straitjacket, so I didn't need blankets. Jasmine slept on the couch next to me to keep an eye on things. She was out in a couple minutes. I was on my back, arms crossed, terrified. I was struck by how difficult it was to breathe. Finding a comfortable position was impossible. Anytime I'd drift off, I was up within minutes. What was I thinking?

In the morning I was cranky, sore, and begging for Jasmine to unstrap me. This was what I'd signed up for? With all the preparation, planning, and theorizing, I'd forgotten about the part where I'd have to spend two weeks in a straitjacket!

Nightmares invaded my slumber over the next few nights. I'd often come to consciousness in a muted-colour reality. Still lying down, I would try to move my head, but my neck wouldn't budge, as though fixed in drying concrete. My eyes would dart from side to side. I would see Jasmine, dressed in black, standing over me, slowly becoming smaller as I'd be lowered into the ground … in a casket. My body would become rigid. I'd smell the wet dirt cascading across my face. Then I'd wake up in the middle of the night, drenched in sweat.

Versions of this dream would replay each night. Men locking me in boxes or tying me up with rope. These fourteen days were going to be interesting for sure.

Jason and I went shopping in preparation for the imminent two weeks. I bought a Bluetooth headset to make phone calls (I'd pick up by shoving my shoulder into my ear) and if I held the button it would activate voice command, meaning I could send tweets, update my Facebook status, or send text messages. We also went to a hardware store and bought hooks and pulleys so I could open doors and pull my pants up and down in the bathroom. We put tape around all the doorknobs so I could bite down and twist them open. The house was reverse toddler-proofed after a long night of finagling.

Jason suggested getting T-shirts with the slogan *"Ask us why he's in it!"* made so that people would feel more comfortable getting information from us. Cheapest meant best, so I bought a bunch of white shirts, cut a stencil out of cardboard, and spray-painted the text myself. Did any of those shirts turn out even a little bit? Sure.[29]

JUNE 30, 2014: One week to go. There were only a few bells and whistles left. I needed a pair of shoes that I could easily slip off to access my toes in emergency situations. A pair of Ralph Lauren loafers did the trick. They were comfortable, and Ralph Lauren was a huge supporter of Parkinson's research. The shoes had a big logo on the front, so anytime my feet were on television I'd be advertising Ralph Lauren and they might pitch some money my way. Maybe? They never noticed my feet on TV (shocker), but they might notice their name in a book.

---

29 Naw.

While I was trying on the shoes, I got a call from my publicist, Marion. Global News wanted me on a segment at six o'clock that night. Prime time. They were going to give me three minutes to plug Escaping Parkinson's and my *Morning Show* visit.

They showed up at my house with cameras to film me doing a few tricks. Afterward, I spoke about the cause and what I was planning.

Jason tweeted about the interview while I gave it. He and Jasmine became my social media team, only Jasmine wasn't able to help at that moment since she was busy moving her family from Kingston to Toronto. When I needed her most! Selfish![30]

We tuned into the six o'clock news and waited. A long time. People were tweeting about not seeing me. Did they cut my segment? Embarrassingly, around 6:50 p.m., there I was. I wonder how many people watched fifty minutes of real news just to see my smug face for five.

Before she went to Kingston, I warned Jasmine that my brain was about to re-enter business mode. I reminded her that this was what had caused the friction between us in the first place.

"Remember, we're not together anymore, so you don't owe me anything. I could really use the help of a best friend," I said. She seemed sadder than I'd anticipated, but she told me that she understood. It was only after I came to terms with the idea of her not loving me that I realized she might still. Oops.

The stunt was five days away and not a single network had shown interest in airing the first day. That's the best part, losers! I called Marion and told her the situation, hoping she'd be able to help. She asked what my backup plan was. I didn't have one. Remember earlier when I spoke to the students about backup plans? I meant that shit.

---

30 Tongue firmly in cheek.

"Mark, I can't get anyone to cover you on the seventh. Maybe you could post the entrance to your YouTube page?" I wanted thousands of people to watch my opening, not hundreds.[31]

"Or … I've spoken to The Morning Show, *and they'd love for you to strap in on their show."* Yes, perfect! Sign me up for the seventh!

"No Mark, you can only get the spot on the eighth. Could you push the stunt a day?"

All my fans had marked July 7th off on their calendars, and the champagne wouldn't be aged correctly if I escaped on the twenty-second instead of the twenty-first. I wasn't willing to admit that no one cared that much, and my stubbornness got in the way. Somehow the offer to strap in live on television didn't click.

"It's going to throw off the timing of everything. Tell them no."

"I think you're making a mistake. If no one covers the first day, you may lose momentum."

"No," I said, *"It's going to throw off the timing."* She told me she'd call *The Morning Show* and relay my wishes before hanging up.

Then I began to pace the train station. Calling Scott would probably give me some confidence in my decision. *"You're an idiot. Take the deal."* I quickly called Marion back.

"Don't worry, Mark. I haven't made the call."

Did I mention I had an amazing team that was way smarter than me?

Global National also asked for a story. They provided news all across Canada. This was the break we needed. They wanted a five-minute spot at six o'clock (on the nose this time). More prime time! They asked to shoot an interview and some footage of me outside, attempting everyday tasks, right after my spot on *The Morning Show.* They said it might be raining, so we'd have to work quickly. *"No problem!"* I said, not bothering to mention that the jacket couldn't get wet or it would likely mold. Things were coming together.

---

31 That's a generous estimate in itself.

I got another call from a TV station in Hamilton, asking me to appear during my second week. Media interest was picking up and stations began securing their spots. As they (I) say, good things happen all at once.

JULY 6, 2014: Two days to go, lying awake, wondering what I'd feel like in two weeks. An urge to back out crept over me. I'd printed off little pieces of paper that had my important health information on them. Every member of my team was required to keep a slip on them at all times. My actual health card lived in the little zippered pocket at the back of my track pants. I never wear track pants, but I was prepared to wear anything comfortable during this process.

Jasmine and Jason sat across from me at my mom's kitchen table. I had planned to give a heroic speech that inspired them both to no end. In reality, our conversation centred on what to do if I was giving up. Begin with the end in mind, right? We developed a code word in case I really needed to call it quits early.

"Do not let me out of this thing unless I say Dakota."

Why Dakota? Because I'd never felt the need to say it before the stunt.

The next morning, I packed my pants, Team Fox shirt, shoes, and earpiece, and my mom drove me to Scott's place just inside Toronto (changing it up). Scott was driving me to the studio early the next morning. Jasmine was moving and Jason would be watching from Oakville; I was allowed one person on set and Scott was the person I needed. We stayed up (too) late and laughed about how much tomorrow was going to suck.

MIDNIGHT, JULY 8, 2014: Reminiscing in the dark. This journey started alone in the main-floor bedroom of my aunt's Montreal home, and now I had a whole team waiting for my launch the next morning. My Facebook was flooded with well wishes. Those personally affected by Parkinson's expressed their support. People who'd lost loved ones or had loved ones currently suffering were sending beautiful words of encouragement. It reminded me that I was doing this for the research. Not the press, money, or kicks, but something bigger.

I made a post thanking all of the people who'd made the stunt possible and took a good look at my hands. I set my phone alarm and lay on the couch, eyes closed, not sleeping. Trying to quiet the butterflies in my stomach. I turned on the fan and tried to relax. It was three in the morning and I couldn't get any rest before the biggest day of my life. At least, despite my stress and nervousness, the universe was still working to its usual standard.

My team and I had run ourselves into the ground for more than a few months, and this project was born. Scott wired money, Jason emailed companies, and Jasmine tried to support me as best she could. It would all start tomorrow. We were all invested in making this thing happen. You either succeed or you stop trying. It's that simple.

DAY 1 - NO TURNING BACK

© Personal Collection
(Scott Hammell)

(And We're Live: Global National films a segment in Scott's house—2014)

JULY 8, 2014: The alarm went off. My heart leapt in my chest. The day had arrived. I ran into Scott's room, apologized to Alex (his startled girlfriend), and woke his ass up. Seeing as it would be my last chance for two weeks, I made sure to shower and shave. Before jumping in the car, I called my mom and told her I loved her (you know, in case this killed me).

We arrived at the studio and an executive led us into TV land. The smell of coffee filled the air. Everyone had a wide morning grin plastered on their face.

He brought us to a beautiful waiting room I called "the holding pen." I could see them shooting in the next room. Scott and I had barely sat down before being greeted by the hosts. They were heavy on the makeup and smiles, but nice enough. One of them really seemed to get a kick out of the stunt. But only one.

Marion, my publicist, arrived for our first face-to-face meeting. Her teeth actually sparkled. They almost hurt to look at. She clearly felt comfortable around the press and that put me at ease. Scott turned on our camera and started asking me questions. I don't remember what I said, but I knew I was thinking, *"Don't screw this up." It was my first on-camera confessional (of what would be many).*

Jasmine was also on my mind. Big time. Was she my soulmate? I tried to quiet my epiphanies long enough to focus on the task at hand.

"Mark, look." Scott pointed to the holding pen monitor: *"Mark Correia up next with Parkinson's campaign."* My name was on television, and I would be next.

They brought me in for hair and makeup, gave me coffee, and made me look beautiful. For once, my hair was the last thing on my mind. The sound guy was wiring me while Scott briefed the main host on how to strap me in. The producers thought an inexperienced anchor sealing my fate for the next two weeks would make for better television. Awesome.

Scott promised to make sure she didn't pull the straps tight enough to involuntarily kill me. Manslaughter seemed inconvenient at this moment.

On in five. Someone told me that if I needed the bathroom, now was the time.

"No, I'm good."

Scott stared at me. *"Dude, this is the last time you'll be able to pee with your hands."*

I went to the bathroom. I probably should've made more of the affair, but I only had two minutes left.[32]

They whisked me onto the set. I shook the hosts' hands again (I had washed them) and sat on my mark. They were shooting in the round, which meant terrible angles for the magic trick they wanted me to perform. Counting down started before I had time to worry.

"Live in five, four, three, two ..." They gave the "one" finger and pointed. Straitjacket standing by.

"Hello! We're live with Mark Correia, who is doing something astounding for Parkinson's research. But first, let's warm up with a card trick." Turn on the charm.

One of the hosts picked a card and shuffled it back into the deck. The card vanished from the deck and reappeared in my pocket. The three of clubs. After some reactions, I revealed that the background photo on my phone was also the three of clubs. They loved it.[33]

I was trying to answer the questions inspiringly, informatively, and comically, without taking any of the spotlight away from the hosts. They don't take kindly to that. Next thing I knew, my arms were being guided into the jacket sleeves. They quickly shot out for one last stretch. As buckles were tightening along my back and my arms were crossing in front of me, the last nine months played back in my head. It all came down to this. This moment—the last moment with my arms for two weeks. Start

---

32 Yes, I suppose that would've been enough time. Ha.

33 It was a shout-out to Penn and Teller. I won't tell you why, but if you watch them do card tricks, you'll understand.

the clock. I don't remember leaving the studio, but I know I didn't shake anyone's hand on the way out.

Now I was in a straitjacket. The glamour continued. *Global National* was waiting to receive me. Before we started the interview, I noticed a familiar face in the holding pen. Ben Mulroney, television personality, and the son of former Prime Minister, Brian Mulroney. You may know him as the host of *Entertainment Tonight*. Canada knows him as one of our four "celebrities."

Jumping on the opportunity, I introduced myself. Suddenly everyone in the studio was interested in me.[34] It probably wasn't often that someone like me was on set. Ben asked why I was wearing a straitjacket (fair question) and kept making jokes about my going to the bathroom. A continuous theme throughout the stunt that never stopped being hilarious, ever.[35]

I asked him if he wouldn't mind signing the jacket and taking a picture together. He agreed. He signed the jacket and a host jumped in for the picture, getting on his tiptoes to match our height. Entertainment egos are so fragile. Ben and I knocked elbows and I thanked him.[36] Lucky break. That signature was good eye candy.[37] Thanks again, Mr. Mulroney!

I got back to my interview with *Global*. The reporter and camera guy were lots of fun. They asked me some serious questions, like, what was I most nervous about? And how would I go to the bathroom? It was around this time I started getting my first itch. I tried to ignore it and continue with my interview. That didn't work. Luckily, they didn't include the shots of me dragging my forehead against the shoulder of the jacket (which also

---

34 Yes. Ben Mulroney was a big deal in Canada. No, really.

35 It's still just as hilarious and original when I hear them today.

36 This was six years before the world collectively switched to this greeting.

37 Yes. In Canada. Really.

didn't work). We wrapped and arranged to meet at Scott's place to shoot me making a sandwich. More performing.

I went back inside and took the elevator down to the parking lot with Scott. My fellow elevator riders made some bathroom comments. Always funny, always fresh. Scott pulled the car around and opened my door so I could get in.

When we arrived at his place, he challenged me to get out of the car. I couldn't quite figure it out. He told me to take off my shoes and use my toes. It was actually pretty frustrating. The door handle just barely clicked open before it slipped from my toes, shutting again. The near completion of tasks would be a reccurring theme for the remainder of the stunt. A theme that would drive me to the brink of insanity.

My shoulders began to ache. This worried me. Three hours and I was already sore. I started some shoulder rotations to get my blood flowing. The effects didn't last long. I also had this torturous impulse whenever the camera stopped rolling: *"Okay, good shot, now let's take off the jacket!"*

Unfortunately, the jacket didn't turn off with the camera. I thought about *The Michael J. Fox Show* and how his character, like him, also had Parkinson's. I wonder if Michael hoped it might turn off with the camera too.

I only ever watched that show for Michael J. Fox and Juliette Goglia. I envied Juliette, who played his daughter. I would kill for the opportunity to be Michael J. Fox's kid, even for a day.[38]

Scott filmed while I ate. I listed the foods that I thought would be easiest to eat. I only got as far as: *"Samosas for the corners, and smoothies."* Scott laughed at me. My plan was to eat smoothies, and only smoothies, for two weeks.

---

38 Juliette, if you are reading this, I'm shooting my shot. Yes, I'm using my book
    as a meet cute.

Scott began to brainstorm, each idea becoming more ridiculous than the last: Eggs and toast smoothies, steak smoothies, mac and cheese smoothies.

"I like smoothies," I said. Deep first-day talk.

I quickly realized that my best tools would be my toes and teeth, although I needed to go easy on the latter. I practiced sending and reading texts with my earpiece's speech feature. A lot of people started following me after seeing *The Morning Show* (on Twitter, not in real life). I posted a status saying there was more to come that afternoon. By the time I hit send it probably said something like, *"Kiss my bum, June!"* This was before Siri and Alexa and Roberto and all that crap.

Just as I was getting comfortable, *Global* showed up. Scott had offered up his kitchen to be destroyed so that they could shoot me making a sandwich. I kept trying to reach out and grab things, only to be thwarted by the canvas covering my arms. Damn. Had to get used to that.

To begin, I opened the fridge with my foot and reached my head into the icy wasteland. I grabbed some ham with my teeth and brought it over to the counter. This worked for everything except the can of soda—my teeth only pushed it farther into the fridge. I struggled with the can until it hit the floor. Picking anything up was an exercise in contortion. It's like trying to pick up a card that's lying flat on the floor and not quite getting your fingernails under it. Except you're using your mouth. Getting back up was a whole separate adventure.

I shoved my face into the bread bag and ripped apart the plastic, along with most of the bread. The meat didn't fare much better. I lay my face on the mustard bottle until it poured onto the sandwich. Voila. This wasn't a pretty sight. To make matters worse, I tried cutting the sandwich in half. I stuck my face in the knife drawer to get a shot (which they didn't end up using) and pushed the knife against the sandwich until it broke through. Somehow, I finished unscathed.

"Can we go film you outside on the street?" In the rain? *"No,"* should have been my answer. My team and I had already agreed to keep the jacket dry. Especially during the first few days.

"Of course!" The camera blinded my judgment. They shot me trying to get out of the house with an umbrella that didn't fit through the door. On the street, I heard them say, *"Make sure to get Ben Mulroney's signature in the shot."* See? I told you!

When we wrapped, my dad picked me up. I was starving when he arrived, so we went to a drive-through for chicken strips—the easiest thing to eat on the menu (they didn't have samosas or smoothies). A friend of mine was working the window. She was more of a friend of a friend, but she grabbed people from the back and brought them forward. They all recognized me from *The Morning Show*. Local celebrity status, unlocked.

Jason was waiting for me when I arrived home. My house became the very messy headquarters of Escaping Parkinson's.

We waited anxiously for everything to air. Jason picked up the camera (which he had never used before) and shot another (out of focus) confessional. This one was about how tired I already was … until … I had to pee. I thought maybe I could get through the stunt without going to the bathroom at all. Not possible apparently. I went to the bathroom and Jason came in to make sure everything went okay. Sounds fun, doesn't it?

Our spot aired. It was great. *Global* ran the segment online with a written story, and Jason tweeted the link. He also tweeted the Ben Mulroney picture, asking if Ben wouldn't mind retweeting it. He answered: *"Of course not! Good luck!!! @Mark_Correia."*[39]

---

39 Now @markclearview for those wishing to follow me.

Jason and I walked to the town plaza, where we usually hung out. The reception was startling. Everyone on the street recognized me as *"That guy from the news!"* Some people asked if I was, in fact, the guy from TV, but others would just start the conversation. *"How much money have you raised so far?"* or, *"How many days has it been again?"*[40] or, *"How's Mr. Fox doing?"* It was kind of overwhelming, so I don't really remember all of the interactions.

It was late on a busy day, so it was time to film a confessional, do my stretches, and plan the next day's events. My nightly confessionals were a good way to sum up the day. So, I did just that: *"If I had to sum up today, I'd call it the first day!"* Today was an easy one, mind you.

I sat next to Jason at my laptop and dictated what to click. Jason compiled suggestions and mapped out what tasks I'd try on which days. We were scheduled to shoot at Dundas Square the following morning because I wanted to interact with the public in the heart of downtown Toronto. I asked my friend Michael to join and hand out print.

Then we began sifting through the day's footage. We'd shot around three hours' worth, so it took until two a.m. to parse through. We sent the chosen clips over to Max to edit. He had until the next afternoon to make something entertaining. It took seven hours to send them over the Internet. We couldn't fit it all in one go, so we set an alarm for four a.m. to wake up and send the next batch. This became a nightly ritual. In the videos, I put on a happy face, but the stunt is over now so I can openly say I really fucking hated doing footage sessions. *"This one is garbage. Send this one. This one can be saved as extra footage. No. The other folder. The other folder. The other, other folder."* I knew if I could take the controls I could do it myself in three seconds. I got impatient. Sometimes, I got ugly. But Jason stayed by my side. *"This clip here? Oh sorry, over here? Here? Here?"*

---

40 The answer was one.

My friends put up with my shit while doing things they had no interest in doing because they cared. They genuinely cared about me and this cause.

I checked my email before bed. I was surprised to see how many people had seen me on TV and taken the time to write. Those messages reminded me why I was doing this.

7.8.14

Mark ... I'm a Parky.

Thanks for this innovative way to raise funds to help deal with this disease. Good luck.

Anonymous

7.8.14

Thanks so much!

I just read about your fundraising for two weeks. Honestly, it brought tears to my eyes seeing the compassion you have. The second to last day of your wearing the straitjacket will be the day my father died one year ago. He had Parkinson's for 25 years. He never complained. He fought with a grateful heart. He was grateful we all stayed by his side and helped all we could. I truly admire your spirit and your compassion. You are an amazing young man. Thank you for raising awareness, raising money, and keeping hope alive for those with PD!

Anonymous

They were just the words I needed.

I collapsed onto the mattress and fell asleep. It had been a successful first day, and I knew it would only get harder from here.

We were in a store looking at mannequins in the window. Jason dared me to put the straitjacket on one of them. One of my friends started undoing the buckles themselves. Guilt began to wash over me slowly. I took off the straitjacket and put it on the mannequin to see if I understood the joke, but I only felt awful. I put it back on quickly, trying to pretend nothing had happened. I was a liar. It was one of the stunt's scariest moments ... until I woke up.

Yes, I just wrote a dream sequence into my book. What are you going to do about it?

DAY 2 - NO APPOINTMENT NECESSARY

(Posers: Posing with Batman in downtown Toronto—2014)

JULY 9, 2014: I groggily rocked myself awake at ten o'clock. My body was locked in one position. It must've been a wild night. Horror struck when I couldn't adjust my neck at all. I was stiff as a board and my shoulder was pulsing. When was the last time you felt your heartbeat in your shoulder? It took me twenty minutes of deliberate stretching to work out the kinks. I noticed Jason missing from the couch and found him sitting behind it on my laptop.[41] He gave me a look that said, *"You're not going to believe this."*

> 7.10.14
>
> Dear Mark,
>
> I was moved and impressed with your straitjacket event to support Parkinson's research.
>
> I have been using the straitjacket example in my presentations to potential investors for the last four years to exemplify the particular symptom of "off" or "freezing" episodes, a symptom of Parkinson's which can affect up to a third of all Parkinson's patients.
>
> Cynapsus recently announced our new delivery method for Apomorphine (the only approved drug in the world that treats the "off" episodes).
>
> Cynapsus will process today or tomorrow a donation of $2,500. Who should the cheque be made out to and where should it be sent?
>
> Keep up the good work.
>
> -Cynapsus Therapeutics Inc.

I was stunned. Day two and we'd already raised seven thousand dollars.

---

41 Working on it, not sitting on it.

Jason came upstairs with me and waited while I used the bathroom. Which was strange. Something was off. I was just about to pee when I caught a glimpse of my reflection in the bowl. I quickly stuck my foot through the toilet seat, crunched my toes, and peeled back a large piece of cellophane. Asshole.

I peed as fast as I could and went to brush my teeth. I accomplished this by taping my toothbrush to the sink beforehand. Now I could squeeze out some toothpaste with my face and move my mouth back and forth around the brush. Clever, right? I pushed my face into the tap for some water, but Jason had rigged the faucet with gum so that it would spray everywhere. Again, asshole. I went to open the door but the tape we'd put on the knob had been removed. Missing tape wasn't about to stop an escape artist. When I finally got out, Jason was giggling like a child. He knew there was nothing I could do to retaliate.

One of our followers had suggested I try to make breakfast, so it seemed like a logical task to start with. I had to try everything myself first. Jason was not to step in. We decided on frozen waffles, but first, orange juice. Scott had given me a bamboo straw to push buttons with and … drink things with (one of the lesser-known uses of the humble drinking straw). I sucked up some juice from the jug and spit it into my cup over and over until it was full. I put the waffles into the toaster with my mouth and angled the toaster so that they popped onto the plate. Then I poured maple syrup over them using my teeth, with surprising success.

I had to go to the bathroom again. This time, I went to the first-floor bathroom. I was just about to pee when I heard Jason's silence in the next room. I put my foot through the seat for good measure. There's no way he woke up early enough to rig both toilets.[42]

---

42 He had.

Jason and I caught the train and made our way downtown. I wouldn't actually be "handing out" anything, but Jason and Michael would. Jason had his *"Ask us why he's in it!"* shirt on and had an extra one for Michael. People came up to us immediately. They came for the straitjacket, but stayed to talk about the project (usually). My heart and soul were in it, and I think people could smell that passion. And I mean that literally.

I took pictures with as many people as I could. The more people I interacted with, the better. I had an online request to do a Michael Jackson impersonation due to my already spot-on impression. Nearby, there was a choir group singing about Jesus. It seemed like the perfect time. Everyone knows that Jesus loved *Thriller*.[43]

I started moonwalking around the choir. They seemed to like it. As I was sidling up to buskers in the street, I recognized a local Toronto celebrity, the Toronto Batman! A man who dresses up in a Batman costume and runs around Toronto "stopping crime" (though he mostly just stands at Dundas Square for pictures). We started battling for the spotlight (aren't performers just so predictable?). I would say something about the stunt, like: *"Be sure to donate to Escaping Parkinson's online!"* and he would reply with: *"MY PARENTS ARE DEAD!"* He answered most questions like that actually. We took a photo together and he told me to post it on his Facebook page. Toronto tries really hard to be New York City. Dundas Square is like Times Square, without the history, the size, or the people, but it's still one of the busiest places in the city. A lot of television networks record there. Citytv, one of the more popular news networks in Canada, has a huge screen where they project their live show. It's kind of the centre of attention in the square. The five o'clock news was coming up (one of the busiest times for foot traffic) and as I stared at the screen, I couldn't help but wonder how to get on it. Jason suggested we pitch our project over the phone, but I had a better idea. I told Michael to stay put in case it worked.

---

43 I wrote this before *Leaving Neverland* came out. I don't actually know if Jesus likes *Thriller*. We've never met.

If people asked who was on the cards he could point to the screen and say, *"That guy."* I got a kick out of that.

Jason and I waited by the door. When someone came out, Jason caught the door and we slithered up to the front desk.

"Hi, my name is Mark Correia and I'm doing a stunt in this straitjacket to raise money for Team Fox. I was wondering if I could get on television?"

The secretary looked at us for a second. *"Have you had any media attention yet?"*

I told her *Global* was all over it, and it would be a real shame if City missed out.

"Okay," she said, *"let me just make a request and send it to the head producer."*

Really? It was that simple? I told her that the jacket had been signed by a couple of celebrities. I only got Ben Mulroney out before she stopped me. Good thing she did, because he was the only "celebrity" who'd signed it.

"Ben Mulroney's signature is on your jacket?"

I showed her the signature and told her about Ben's tweet wishing us luck. I kept referring to Jason as my cameraman, to make us seem official. She gained interest with each question we answered. Maybe this was working? She stopped me when we mentioned the quote from Michael J. Fox.

"Let me see if I can get someone from upstairs to talk to you." That'd be great. As luck would have it, an anchor walked through the front door at that exact moment. The secretary called him over.

"Roger! You have to see this kid. Look at his straitjacket. It's signed by Mulroney. It's all for Parkinson's research."

He looked at me. *"Oh, you got Ben? Gimme a pen."* He grabbed a sharpie and wrote: *"YOU'RE NUTS! But for a good cause!"*

Then he said, *"You wanna be on the five o'clock news?"*

"It would be my pleasure."

We followed him into the elevator. Did I just walk onto the news?[44]

---

44 That's right, kids. Go bug your local news stations. Instagram fame is a thing of the past.

Roger introduced me to the segment producer, and I told her my story. She took pictures of me for Twitter and said, *"Can you come back at around five-forty? You're going to be on near the end of the broadcast."* Even better.

They took all my information and started putting together graphics for the show. I met another anchor whom I recognized from television. She was the one I'd be on the air with. She was very down-to-earth and articulate (basically, her job). She gave me her card and told me if I needed anything throughout the stunt, I could message her. Jason and I bumped elbows and went downstairs to find Michael.

We told Michael everything. He suggested we get a bite in the mall and come back closer to game time. So, we went to a fast-food restaurant. I had a strip of Velcro on the front of the jacket and another strip on my wallet. Cashiers would rip the wallet off my chest and tap my card themselves. Yay capitalism!

After struggling with scalding hot fries, we took our positions for the news. Michael on the street and Jason and me on our way upstairs. We were shown to a beautiful holding pen to take some photos. Jason tweeted the news and I called Marion. She couldn't believe it either. There was a whiteboard in the room with: *"Discussion on future segments"* written on it. Jason wrote: *"Escaping Parkinson's should come back."* You have to be creative to be noticed.

As quickly as I'd arrived upstairs, the cameras were rolling. My shoulders were in immense pain, but I wanted to be as personable as I could. They mentioned that one of the anchors had found me wandering the lobby and decided to take me up. Funny when you hear it out loud.

Jason was filming clips for our daily video. Michael was on the street, handing out postcards to people. As they looked up from their card to the screen, they thought a little harder about us and our cause. And that was good enough for me.

After I finished posing for pictures, Michael invited us over for dinner. I was going to shove my head into the plate right in front of his mother, like a horse into a trough, and that amused me. Thinking back on it, we should've just strapped a horse feeder to my face for the whole stunt. Michael told me he had a gadget called "The Thumper" at his house. I told him that if it wasn't an intimate toy, I'd be delighted to see it.[45]

When we arrived, his lovely mother, Karen, prepared a meal that Michael was forced to feed me. I was getting fed up with the jacket impeding on mealtime. We then went downstairs, and Michael pulled out a device with two balls on the end of a stick that vibrated. Skeptical, I let him put it on my shoulder. It began to pound my flesh, and oh boy did it feel like magic.[46]

Michael offered a place to crash, but I didn't feel comfortable sleeping outside the house yet. To be honest, I was scared. I wanted my familiar floor and mattress. Jason and I caught the train back home, uploaded the day one video, and went through the new footage. *"If I had to sum up today, I'd call it the sweaty day."*

The doorbell rang. Jasmine. Home from moving.

She was excited to see me, and very worried by my already ragged appearance. As soon as she was inside, she started talking about her moving fiasco. I was interested, I really was, but I had a hard time showing it. It had been a very long day and my eyes were getting heavy. Jasmine was clearly disappointed. She wanted to debrief with her best friend, but I wasn't great company. I apologized. She said it was okay and managed a smile. At least our team was whole again.

---

45 I would have seen it either way.

46 I don't use this term lightly.

DAY 3 - I'M DECOMPOSING

(Breakfast: Making pancakes—2014)

JUNE 10, 2014: It was clear that I had a problem when I woke up. My hands had developed a waxy texture, like a layer of film had grown over them. A bacterium buildup had begun. My hands weren't just dirty, they were decomposing. I called Scott and asked if this was a health concern.

"Yes, it's definitely a concern," he said. *"I figured you'd thought of that?"*

How hadn't I? The jacket smelled. Especially in the sleeves. Three days in and my hands were posing the biggest threat to the completion of the stunt.

"What if we used hand sanitizer?" Scott proposed. *"Like, fed some thick tubing down the neck hole, and poured some into your palms?"*

We hopped into Mom's car and drove to the closest convenience store. No tubing. Jasmine called our attention to a skipping rope, a green tube with pink handles.

"Jas, this is a skipping rope. It's too thin." She bet fifty dollars toward the foundation that it would work. We bought it and drove home. Jasmine cut the handles off and tried feeding one end through the neck and down the sleeve. It was like threading a needle. You get close, sure, but the thread slips at the last moment, leaving you where you started. The longer it goes on, the more frustrated you become. Or the more frustrated the needle becomes? I don't understand my own analogies. Anyway, we finally got the tube in my hand and painfully attempted to pour the sanitizer down. It would be months before a drop actually hit my fingers. The tube was too thin. Ha. As I prepared to collect the money, Jasmine had a stroke of genius. She put one end of the tube into the bottle, and the other in her mouth, sucking the sanitizer into the tube. This time she threaded the tube between the back buckles and straight into my hand. I grabbed the end, and she blew it out. The solution was in my hands. She pulled the tube out triumphantly and took a bow. Not so fast! My hands were sticky! She repeated the process again with water and told me to shut up. My hands felt moist and alive again. She donated the fifty dollars anyway.

This provided a few hours of relief, and so it became another nightly ritual. Some days my hand would obstruct the end of the tube and Jasmine would almost pop her lymph nodes blowing the sanitizer out. That's love.

Equipped with clean hands and a better attitude, I set out to make some pancakes. It was a suggested challenge, yes, but mostly I just wanted pancakes. I opened the fridge. No maple syrup. Oh, the humanity! The perfect excuse to go to the store and do some filming.

Almost everyone in line recognized me. Little did I know, the newspaper had featured Escaping Parkinson's on the front page that morning. Combine that with the five o'clock news the night before and we'd created the perfect storm for local visibility. It all culminated into one of my favourite moments.

I bought my maple syrup and started walking back to the house. Jasmine agreed to record while Jason stayed home and stirred the mix. She happened to be filming when two young girls, maybe eight or nine years old, walked by. One of them screamed, *"HEY!"* so I turned around to greet them.

They were very cute and overexcited. *"You're the guy from the newspaper!"* Their mother asked if they could take a picture with me. I found out they were twins and that it was their eleventh birthday. I was happy to contribute some fun to it. As we walked away, we heard a loud shriek behind us. *"OH MY GOD!"* they screamed. Step aside, Bieber.

When I got home, I discovered another bodily problem. My left shoulder was making a loud clicking noise whenever I shifted positions. Not a great sign for the escape or for my general wellbeing. I would've appreciated the added dramatic effect if it wasn't so painful; it sounded like somebody was popping corn in my rotator cuff. I figured it would stop eventually.[47]

I was able to ignore my shoulder long enough to flip some pancakes perfectly, spatula in mouth. Most of the tasks turned out better than I expected. Sometimes my friends would help behind the scenes for getting

---

47 It didn't. It still clicks today.

the right ratio of milk and such—cutting back to me for the funny stuff—but a lot of the tasks were accomplished completely on my own. Most meals turned out pretty good, if I do say so myself. My friends may disagree, but fuck'em. What did they ever do? I flipped both pancakes, got them on a plate, covered them in syrup, and ate them. I may have choked on a whole egg trying to suck it out of the carton, but who hasn't?

That evening, my life became a little more frustrating. The cause: minigolf. I'm very competitive when it comes to minigolf.[48] No one actually enjoys this sport,[49] I know, but if you're not of drinking age in Oakville you only have a few options for a night on the town: the movies, minigolf, or both. You can imagine how lucky my middle school girlfriends were. I'm not sure what the minigolf playing space is called, actually. The arena? The field? The green? Anyway, me, Jasmine, and Jason made our way to the front desk and asked if they would give us a discount due to the charitable nature of our stunt. The woman behind the counter let us in for free.

I managed to get one over par on the first hole by feeding the club between my arms and throwing my torso to the side. Maybe this wouldn't be so hard after all.

I was adding strokes on every hole, my internal rage growing until I was eventually wailing on the ball. Imagine a little white speck bouncing off the scenery, over your head, and then: *"FUCK!"* You avert your attention to a poorly shaved teenager in a straitjacket. It was a memorable night at Putting Edge!

This was my social fate for the next eleven days. I could try to deny it, but I wasn't a regular kid anymore. Most of the time I just sat around and watched, playing mental games and reciting song lyrics in my head. Jason got a hole in one on the last hole. I don't remember how many strokes it

---

48 And everything else, but mostly minigolf.
49 Calling minigolf a sport is like calling a poker player an athlete.

took me, but my final score was seventy-eight. I was beginning to notice a learning curve. A curve I was on the wrong side of.

Sitting on the curb, waiting for my mom to pick us up, I filmed a confessional about the experience. My earpiece was starting to hurt my ear. They're not designed to be worn for long periods of time, but I figured it would be the least of my worries in a straitjacket. For some reason, I challenged myself not to take it off before the end of the day. I was stubborn, okay? It kept my mind off the pain in my shoulder anyway, which was growing exponentially.

Sending the daily footage via the Internet was taking way too long, so Max suggested we rotate SD cards in the mailbox. Our method was as follows: Jason would transfer the SD card from the camera to the laptop, I would dictate which clips to keep, and Jasmine would run it to the mailbox. Max would then pick it up, edit, and upload the video, then replace the now empty card in the mailbox when he picked up the next one. If you think that was complicated to read, imagine orchestrating it. We had more than one argument over which card had what footage. It's a miracle we never deleted anything by accident. Equally as annoying, but far quicker than sending it online.

7.10.14

Hey! I think what you're doing is amazing! A really close person in my life is suffering from one of the most severe cases of Parkinson's right now, so I very much enjoy this project. Hope you finally get some freedom back!

-Anonymous

It was around one a.m. and I was ready to crash. The stunt was taking off online, and I was surrounded by people I loved. This thing was working. There wasn't a doubt in my mind that my stunt would be a wild success. All my planning was worthwhile. My dream was coming true. I was getting the attention I deserved. Me, me, me.

Little did I know that everything was going to take a turn for the worse. Sure, we were all motivated, but the jacket was taking its toll.

DAY 4 - A DICK ON ROLLER SKATES

© Personal Collection
(Jason D'Souza)

(Liability Issue: Scooter's Roller Palace, Oakville—2014)

JULY 11, 2014: I'd had enough. This was unfortunate, considering that there were still ten days left. I remember telling my friends I needed out soon. There wasn't much they could do. Funnily, this was also the day I realized I wouldn't quit. I was going to finish this thing and meet our goal if it killed me.

I noticed some Canadian celebrities had been tweeting with the hashtag *"#escapingparkinsons."* It was trending on Twitter now. We also had a whole new pack of names to add to the straitjacket. We took a picture of the names and shared it on Instagram.

I was challenged to take a selfie by a fan. He told me that if I took one successfully, he would donate. This was the first challenge of many where someone would only donate if I completed the task. It really upped the incentive. I took a great selfie with my foot, and he coughed up.

While my jacket added a physical layer to my body, it removed an internal layer: my filter. It brought out a temper I hadn't before confronted, causing me to lash out at the people around me (unfortunately, the people I loved most). I was short with Jasmine. *"Do this quicker, pick that up faster, feed me better."* It really felt like nobody around me was doing anything right. If I could only use my hands, I could fix the problems that were so clear to me, and me only.

I felt sick. My shoulder was killing me. The pain was constant. I was a victim of the stunt I'd created and was being a dick about it.[50] In truth, I didn't like who I was becoming around them, and it only made it harder to be around myself.

---

50 Don't ask Jasmine. She'll tell you I already was.

I was challenged to make an omelette. After all, you have to break a few—I don't feel like completing this joke.

I broke a few eggs on the rim of the bowl using my mouth and blew into the egg until the insides shot into the bowl. With a whisk between my teeth, I beat them together. I used my foot to take a frying pan out of the bottom drawer and throw it onto the counter. With my face, I adjusted the pan on the hot element (safety first). I bit onto the rim of the bowl, tilted my head, and poured the eggs in. Again, shocking success. I'm surprised I never chipped a tooth. The cheese was cut by pressing the side of my face into the back of a knife (again, safety first). I dropped little pieces of cheese into the middle of the egg, and even folded it with the spatula between my teeth. Breakfast was served.

If I were to do anything differently, I probably would have attempted messier tasks. There were a couple I never got around to, like changing a tire on a car, or baking a cake from scratch. I put off the messy ones because I didn't want to ruin the jacket early. I expected it to be filthy by the last day. Don't get me wrong, it's very dirty, it smells worse than a gym full of horses, but I was hoping for more stains. Anyway, I'm sure I have bigger regrets than the cleanliness of my jacket ... and I'm sure we'll get to them.

Some people in an online magic forum suggested I set up a large banquet table. It proved difficult to get a dining room table's worth of dishes that I could smash on a low budget. My mom was delighted when I chose to just shoot it at home.[51] I got a glass I didn't care about breaking and Jasmine cleared a spot on the floor where it could shatter. We made it seem like I was planning on setting the whole table when a glass fell accidentally and caused me to call the whole task off. So admittedly, we set this one up, but I really wanted to break something (besides my interpersonal relationships).

---

51 Just kidding. She didn't know.

Cleaning up the bits of glass wouldn't be easy in a straitjacket. Luckily, Jasmine and Jason stepped in, totally of their own accord, I might add. Completely. They were happy to sweep up my mess. No, really.

7.11.14

I am an Oakville resident and I have a friend in town who is suffering from early-onset Parkinson's. I would love if we could meet you either today or Sunday to sign your straitjacket and put it on YouTube. It would mean a lot to her to know others are making changes for this challenging disease, and something that would be a great gift to her.

- Jackie Patrick

This email right here is what the stunt was about. We went for lunch in the area and waited for Heidi and the Patricks to arrive (Jackie was to be accompanied by her family). I decided to tackle the challenge of eating sushi with chopsticks while I waited.[52] The budget for classy Japanese cuisine was nonexistent, so I went to the grocery store for some prepackaged sushi and sat in a restaurant with nondescript decor. I popped open the lid to the package, realizing I'd forgotten chopsticks. I decided on drinking straws to save the day. But I got frustrated and ended up just shoving my face into it. Another task that could've used more planning. I think we missed a good opportunity on that one.

This was the most nervous I'd been all week. I was actually meeting a member of the community for whom my stunt aimed to benefit. What if she thought I was doing this for the wrong reasons? What if I said

---

52 Thanks to Charlotte Brown for the suggestion.

something insensitive? What if I had sushi on my face? I scarfed down the roll to settle my nerves.

Meeting them was a high point. Jackie was happy to be involved in any way she could. She donated one hundred dollars, even though I told her she could sign the jacket for free. When I met Heidi, I became surprisingly self-conscious about everything I was saying. I knew about Parkinson's disease, but would I know enough? Could I, someone without Parkinson's, ever know enough?

She signed the jacket, at first with steady hands, but then whenever her motion stopped the tremors began to show. She revealed how much medication she was on in order to simply sign her name. The symptoms were there, but what I was really looking at was her face. She was smiling. Medicated to function in a way I took for granted. Smiling. Parkinson's disease is not abstract. It isn't a qualifier for a magic stunt. It's very real, and it involves someone slowly losing authority over their body. It was important to remember that. To wake up with PD every single morning and smile in the face of it, to me, is real bravery.

Millions of people around the world don't have the option to loosen the straps. The courage of people like Heidi was my inspiration. Without real heroes like her, we wouldn't have performative ones like me.

Are you an underage teenager in Oakville? Tired of minigolf/movie dates with magicians? Scooter's Roller Palace is the place for you! Put on some roller skates, listen to songs from the '70s, and skate in a circle! Perfect for an idiot in a straitjacket.

My mother drove us to Scooter's and I went inside to ask some questions. The owner told us we couldn't film his guests, but if it was for charity we could come back at midnight and he would keep the doors open for an extra fifteen minutes. The gang and I bumped elbows and went home to kill time.

Michael was crashing at my place that night so he could tag along on the adventure we'd planned for the next morning. Jasmine and I snuck upstairs for a bit while we waited. It was the first time we'd been alone in a week. We may have kissed for the first time in months. Whatever we did, I didn't use my hands. Michael arrived around eleven-thirty. He was coming from a wedding and didn't have a change of clothes, so we loaded his ass into the car, suit and all.

We were in for a bit of a surprise when we arrived. The owner had changed his mind. He realized that somebody sliding all over a hard surface in a straitjacket, capable of cracking their skull, might be a liability issue. I tried my best to charm him, but he said there was no way I could skate on the rink.

"Hey!" I said, *"Wouldn't it make sense if we stayed on the carpet?"* He looked confused.

"One: not slippery, and two: soft landing!" Surprisingly, he agreed. While Jason put my skates on, I looked into the camera lens and said, *"Jason was hired solely to put my shoes on ... Solely."*[53]

I was bummed that I wasn't actually going to skate. As far as I was concerned, getting hurt was the whole idea.

Like I mentioned before, the desire to be the prime focus: Big character flaw. But I genuinely don't care if people are laughing with me or at me, as long as they're laughing. I don't know if it's a need to feel loved, or to see the smiles I can't always drum up in myself. What I do know is that there is an undying need to entertain, no matter the means. (That's the best I could come up with, so throw some quotation marks around it and post it on your blog, okay?)

To make a long story short, I couldn't get the skates to cooperate. I took a tumble (which may or may not have been intentional) and I needed help. Michael tried to pick me up by my armpits. I put my feet on the ground, without noticing my knees shoot directly into his groin. The more he tried to move me, the more I slid around. When he finally lifted me straight

---

53 Because shoes have soles.

up, my feet hit the floor and splayed out in opposite directions. It was an unplanned *Three Stooges* routine … with two stooges.

It's these moments that I most want to remember. Ten minutes of falling down and laughing with my friends. The moments when we'd stop worrying about public image, likes, money, and became teenagers for a while. No matter how much we've changed over the years, I will always think back on these moments with fondness. Remarkable memories with my closest friends—a gift I was not expecting from this experience.

We waited for my mom outside Scooter's. Without my arms to balance, I just about toppled over while trying to sit down on the curb. It was these brief annoyances that transformed into full-blown bad moods. I was feeling less like myself. I could feel muscle spasms beginning. Though the lack of motor control was concerning, I kept it to myself. I didn't want anyone getting worried and pulling the plug.

I would fall asleep that night, as I did every night, thinking about Jasmine. There was undeniable tension between the two of us. I loved her, she loved me, but we were never clear on where we stood. First and foremost, she was my best friend, which came with its own set of consequences. She'd hear all the thoughts and worries I didn't share with anyone else. Not even Jason. Which meant that she also dealt with the side of me I didn't want to share at all.

Jason was busy the next day, so we took him home and headed back to my place. I had to … sit down … if you know what I mean. It took an impressive four days and low-fibre diet, but I couldn't hold it any longer. It was a production. Half an hour's worth. I'll outline the process as much as I can, because I know it's the main reason you bought this book.

I entered the bathroom. Jasmine did something to give me a little more "room." I slid certain things down, positioned myself on the good side of the toilet, and went … . Then, I employed my cleaning method, which could be done completely alone with duct tape, a plastic bag, and a strip of toilet paper. I admit that I sometimes put my friends to use, so sue me![54] I'd put everything back in place after, remaining strapped in the jacket the whole time.

After relieving myself, I needed sleep. We had quite the task on our hands the next day. I finished going through the footage with Jasmine, rolled off the couch, and landed on my bed. I heard Michael and Jasmine's continued laughter as I drifted off.

---

54 They might.

DAY 5 - 'HOLD ON'

© Personal Collection
(Jason D'Souza)

(Happy as Ever: Canada's Wonderland—2014)

This chapter comes with a built-in drinking game. Take a shot each time you see the words "hold on." (Yes, the ones I just wrote count.) While you're at it, why not write a review of my book eight shots deep? I'm significantly more hilarious when my audience is drunk.

JULY 12, 2014: I woke up cranky, but it wasn't time for emotions. It was time for Canada's Wonderland, Canada's largest amusement park. It features the eighth tallest roller coaster in the world, the Leviathan. The perfect place to go when you've been challenged to ride a roller coaster. The park opens at ten in the morning and closes at ten at night. The goal is to stay all day in order to get your money's worth. I was excited, but that may have been a front to hide the nerves. I put on my earpiece and tweeted my plans, tagging @canadaswonderland. I'd done this before to no avail, along with calling guest services, reaching only an answering machine. Apparently, this tweet warranted the response: *"Have fun Mark! What exactly are you planning?"* I didn't answer.

I knew they wouldn't let me through in a straitjacket, but I thought we would at least get a funny video out of it. Driving all the way to Wonderland with packed lunches just to be sent home. Ha.

We had packed sandwiches, soda, and peaches. I was about to take on the most requested task. Unfortunately, Wonderland is a money pit. Season passes cost seventy dollars (on sale); parking is twenty dollars for the day, priority parking is twenty-five dollars; the food in the park is twenty dollars per meal; bottled water costs four dollars; a line-jump pass is an extra sixty dollars; some of the bigger rides can cost an extra thirty dollars, and souvenirs are out of the question. Pretty soon you're mortgaging your house in order to give your kids a reason to love you.

Our crew included my dad, Michael, Jasmine, and Scott. My dad loves roller coasters, Scott jumps out of airplanes, and Michael is as stupid as I am. Jasmine was the wild card.

You see, Jasmine and I used to go to Wonderland together as children, despite both being afraid of roller coasters. We'd always agree not to force one another onto any rides we were scared of. But by the end of the day, we'd end up pushing each other onto the very rides that terrified us the most. As soon as we were facing our fears, we were in charge of those fears. This always inspired me, and I soon became engrossed in conquering things I was afraid of.

We hit the parking lot and walked to the front gate. Hundreds of heads turned in synchronization. Some folks held their children closer. Some began to laugh. The five of us began to smile.

Every member of my team was wearing their *"Ask us why he's in it!"* shirt, and was equipped with enough print for the whole park. I posed for my pass picture and awaited the moment of truth. Would they take it? The photographer began questioning me. But it was only genuine curiosity. My dad told him the whole story and gave him a card. He asked to take a picture *with* me. This was going better than I thought! We took a few more pictures with the staff and I got my pass. Would security be so understanding? I went through the metal detector with Scott behind me. Then I was in the park. What?

The only thing concerning me now was which ride to go on first. The biggest ride, Leviathan, is complete with a 305-foot-high drop. I wanted to start smaller, so I made my way toward the ride Jasmine and I used to start with, the Vortex. This ride would give me the energy I needed. On our way there we got distracted by an even smaller ride, and picked that one. Jas was already nervous.

Our biggest question was how to actually film my experience on the rides. We figured out that if we had people on the sidelines with cameras, and snuck a GoPro onto the smaller rides, we'd actually have a shot at capturing it.

I rushed past the operator and took my seat. *"Please don't notice me, please don't notice me."* Scott got in next to me, Jasmine and Michael got in the car behind us. My dad was filming things from the ground. The ride operator looked right at me and froze. Her associate was coming around, pulling down the lap bars. As he pulled ours down, she looked directly at me and said, *"All clear."* The ride pulled out of the gate. I couldn't believe it!

I held eye contact with the associate until she disappeared from view. Fear set in. I was about to ride a roller coaster in a straitjacket. We climbed above the park—*click, click, click.* People on the ground were pointing. Michael took out his cell phone and started filming (don't worry, it was a BlackBerry).

The first drop approached.

Click.

My arms were forced into my chest as we fell, crushing my ribs. We started whipping around corners, picking up speed as we went. It was so much fun; I hardly noticed my bad shoulder smashing into Scott's bad shoulder. Before I knew it, the ride was over. I walked off, a little shaken, and looked at my team. The sensation was terrifying, but that's what made it worth it. I understood why Scott took such big risks all the time. If people worried a little less about dying and a little more about living, I wouldn't be so worried about wasting ink on this fucking cliché.

I noticed a lot of people talking about someone they'd seen on television. Then I realized it was me.

"Hey! You're the straitjacket guy! How's it going?" And then of course, *"How do you go to the bathroom?"*

Someone put ten dollars in Scott's hand and wished us luck, without asking any questions. Almost everyone in the park wanted a picture. This was cool at first, but it quickly lost its allure. It took us twice as long to get from ride to ride. At the same time, I wanted to thank everyone who took an interest. Lots of people tweeted those pictures later, thanking us back.

Apparently, teenage girls are also interested in straitjackets?[55] (Or magicians.)[56] Jasmine didn't try to hide her jealousy, and I can't blame her for it. We weren't a couple anymore, but we were the "in-between" thing. Everyone knows a mildly attractive boy in medical gear is Wonderland's *greatest* attraction. This was especially true of a group of girls on a trip from Michigan. They kept asking about my charity work and taking my picture. I noticed Jasmine's face and recognized that someday soon I was going to be the lonely boy off to the side. I thanked the group for their interest, and walked over to sit with her.

Scott and I were in line for the Vortex when the stares began to feel different. Wait a second, I thought, this wasn't fame. I was a freak! A sideshow attraction. I was no movie star; I was the kid who wore a cape to school. A critical hit to my ego.

I started worrying that the attention might draw security's attention. The grounds were getting busier as we entered theme park rush hour. I doubted that the attendants would take kindly to a five-minute speech about Parkinson's and why it had anything to do with roller coasters. I pushed my luck and waited for the front car. When it arrived, Scott and I shuffled in. The restraint was a shoulder bar this time, so they really had to work to get that last click over my crossed arms. I wasn't going to fall out of the ride, but I also wasn't going to breathe. We didn't even get a look from the ride attendant. He gave his thumbs up and away we went.

Here are some tips to have more fun on roller coasters: Play go fish on the climb up and lose the entire deck on the drop. Unbuckle the safety restraint and jump off the side. Both thrilling ideas, but all I had this time was a straitjacket and my screams.

---

55 Nope.

56 Also incorrect.

We dropped. My stomach hit my mouth. Scott was giggling like a toddler with a lolly. When the coaster screeched to a stop, my brain rattled inside my head. Mission accomplished.

I wanted one of those drink hats, so I bought one for twenty-five dollars. It worked, but I guess pink-drink-hat demand was down because the tubes had been collecting dust and that dust was delivered straight to my mouth with each sip. When I spit it out, the water continued pouring out of the tubes and onto my shoulder. The jacket got wet and I was out twenty-five dollars.

I was beginning to think ride operators didn't even know what a strait-jacket was. They kept letting me through without asking any questions. They must've thought it was for medical protection or something. They clicked down the arm bar and away we went. I puffed out my chest to avoid slipping out. The ride slowly came to a stop and the bars popped open. There was relief in my shoulder for the first time. I felt bliss.

Next, Windseeker: a 301-foot pole equipped with an ascending carousel of chairs. That's it. No drop, no surprises, no speed. Just height. How bad could it be? Michael smuggled Scott's GoPro into the line and waited. Jasmine and Scott were bonding, so I let them be. He's very hard not to look up to (despite his height, or lack thereof) and I wanted Scott to understand how lucky I was to have her, why I'd been fighting so hard to keep her. She had her own fucking amazing life outside of mine, and was only taking a short break to scratch my butt and stuff. This was the sentimental rumination I was having while trying to focus on not shitting my pants in line. When we hit the gates to get on, the attendants just looked at me and laughed. *"Good luck holding on!"* Not what you want to hear before getting on an amusement park attraction.

The ride was so tall I could feel the wind moving the pole we were attached to. It was petrifying. I couldn't focus on the pain in my arms because I was too worried about falling to a certain death … but wow, the view was pretty. Michael took out the camera, clasped it between his hands, and pointed it at me while I spouted my daily confessional. Paralyzed with fear.

Back on the ground, I made a break for the Vortex. It was my favourite rollercoaster and I was going to ride it more than once. Upfront. With my best friend.

Jas and I waited for the front car. One of the attendants came around, pulled down the chest bars, gave a thumbs up, and we were on our way. Before stopping abruptly. I was so excited I barely noticed.

"Excuse me, sir?"

I didn't notice the attendant, so Jasmine hit me. *"What? Yes?"*

"You need arms for this ride." I have arms.

"I've ridden this before."

"No sir, you need to hold on. I can't launch the ride until you hold on."

"No, really, I just rode this like ten minutes ago and it was fine."

"Listen, you can't ride in that. You'll have to take it off."

If only.

Miraculously, the previous attendant came over. *"Hey, he rode like ten minutes ago. He's fine."*

She looked at us for a moment. *"Okay, have fun, but you shouldn't be on the ride."* She gave a thumbs up and off we went.

We had similar troubles later on.

"Sir, you can't ride like that. You need to hold on."

This time Jasmine piped in. *"We get this a lot. He's fine. You can start the ride."*

Not the greatest sales pitch.

"Um. No. He can't ride if he can't hold on. Period."

"What she means is, we just got this from the Vortex, but I've ridden it twice and they seemed okay with that. Think it's just a misunderstanding."

"It isn't a misunderstanding. We just can't start the ride if you're not holding on."

"Look, nobody holds on anyway. If the ride was that dangerous—"

"Sir I'm asking you to get off."

"What? No, I won't. I mean, I can't. I was let into the park this morning, I paid for this, I—"

Jasmine: *"We bought season passes."*

A scene was brewing.

"It doesn't matter if you bought passes. You can't hold on. If you don't get off, no one is riding."

Michael: "Mark, I don't think it's gonna happen this time."

Me: *"Are you serious?"*

Attendant: *"Yes."*

Me: *"Okay. It's fine. Sorry about that. Have fun, everyone."*

Jasmine leapt off, smiling. Solidarity? Maybe. Although she was probably just happy that she was off the ride. I, on the other hand, was mad. Mostly because I knew I was in the wrong. They were just doing their job, and I was shouting about getting seven chicken nuggets instead of eight. Wait, could I be learning something? Was I just told I wasn't able to do something and there was nothing I could do about it? Maybe I wasn't used to that in my privileged upbringing. Not like this anyway. How lucky was I? Only nine more days for me. For some people, this was an inescapable reality. Humbled, I cooled off from my tantrum.

When the ride was over, Michael and Scott went on about how much they hated it. Either it was *actually* that hard on the neck, or they were just being good friends. I couldn't tell.

Jasmine wanted to ride a roller coaster where you lie flat on your stomach. I sat this one out to catch my breath.

I was still arguing with the attendant in my head when I noticed a security guard on a walkie-talkie. I turned away and started conversing with Scott, to prove I wasn't in this garb out of necessity. She walked toward us. *"Shit."*

Scott turned on the camera as the security guard approached.

"Why are you wearing a straitjacket?" she asked.

I happily explained and Scott gave her a card. She didn't look at it.

"You can't wear that in the park." We were a bit shocked.

"Then how am I in the park?" (Not only did security let us through, they'd actually taken pictures with us, remember?)

She persisted. *"I'm sorry about that, but you'll have to leave immediately."*

We continued to explain the situation (less happily), how we weren't going to leave the park, how I paid to get in, and how I clearly wasn't disturbing anyone.

"You're allowed to stay, but the straitjacket will have to leave." Scott informed her that while I'd love that, I wasn't able to remove it for another nine days.

She switched angles. *"I understand. It's just something we don't recognize in our park. It's a red flag for our security. I've called my superiors, but personally, I think it's a really great thing what you guys are doing."*

Heartwarming support from a security guard whose personal mission was to remove magicians from amusement parks.

Jasmine and Michael approached as people around us began taking pictures. Jasmine didn't miss a beat. *"Is there a problem here?"*

The eliminator of magical threats explained that we had to leave.

"Why?" said Jasmine.

Just then, the head security guard appeared with two more guards as backup. We now had a ring of security around us. Scott broke out the big guns.[57] He outlined the negative message this would convey about mental illness, and how bad it would look to kick out spokespeople for the Michael J. Fox Foundation. My dad pulled out his phone and showed

---

57 Metaphorical guns. Actual guns would've escalated the situation.

them all the news stories we'd been featured on. The head guard agreed to call the head of security. This was getting ridiculous. My team was filming everything. There was also an outer ring of park patrons forming, asking what was going on (perfect opportunity to explain the stunt).

The woman in charge showed up. *"I think we have a misunderstanding. I understand you're performing in the park to promote something?"*

We all explained that I wasn't performing in the slightest. My team members weren't strangers to me performing. This was not that. She offered to call up the chain of command to see what the people upstairs had to say. Go for it.

Scott told her, *"This is going to end very negatively for one of us … and I have a feeling I know who it will be."*

At that moment, a little girl and her mother came over to greet me. *"We both watched you on TV last night, and were wondering if we could get a picture with you."* Perfect timing. I posed and started making the girl laugh. With her laughing and her mom filming, I knew they couldn't get rid of us.

The security brigade came back from their collective phone call. *"Okay, so we called up the ladder and have good news! You get to stay in the park, ride the rides, and hand out your print. Have a wonderful day at Wonderland!"* Shocker.

Before leaving us, the head of security paused and said, *"Can I actually get a picture with you to show my kids?"*

She huddled up next to me and added, *"My name is Sarah, let me know if you need anything."*

Thanks, Sarah. We need lunch.

We walked to the front gates, and the man stamped my ankle as I exited. We were buzzing about the incident as we approached the car with our perfectly packed lunches. We ate our sandwiches in the sun, beaming at our victory.

I was getting a craving for dessert when funnel cakes caught my eye (they often do). Michael went over to get some. I told him I wanted strawberries on top and ice cream on the side. Michael thought the ice cream was a bad idea considering whenever I had milk, I got gassy and shat everywhere. True, but I wanted it anyway. Michael argued that we didn't want to take any chances and that I wouldn't be the one cleaning up the mistake. I didn't get any ice cream.

As we were walking to the tables, I tried to sneak a bite of Michael's ice cream. I thought it would be funny, and it was awfully hot outside. He hit me over the head to stop me. Now, this had happened hundreds of times before, and usually I just laugh it off. This time, however, I felt the back of my neck get hot. Rage. I'm sure if we had been out of sight of potential donors I would have snapped. I honestly don't remember how I kept myself together. Somehow, I managed to clench my jaw shut, walk away, and have a moment of meditation to myself. Jasmine noticed something was up and came over after a few minutes. Before I had a chance to take it out on her, she ran her fingers through my hair and told me that whatever I was feeling was temporary. Holy shit. That did the trick.

While I was away having my moment, Michael told Scott that it was not wise to let me eat any ice cream because of my bowels. Clearly, he had more lactose intelligence than I did. So, Scott began filming as I returned to our table. I looked from one friend to the next. There was an arch in my eyebrow. If I had use of my hands, I would've been wringing them ominously. After a moment of silence, I dove directly into Michael's plate, ice cream flying everywhere. He put his hand over his face, but you can still make out the look of horror in everyone's eyes in the video.

After my face was good and covered, Scott's jaw dropped.

"Oh my god, it's Adam Sandler!"

I flipped; work mode. Quick, clean me up! Get a sharpie! Maybe he'd post a photo of us. Imagine the donations!

"I'm fucking with you," he said. Ice cream dripped down my chin. That is what friends are for.

What is the most frustrating carnival game to play without hands? Ring toss. Obviously. It's frustrating *with* them. Everyone knows the bottles are too close together. They even have the audacity to colour code them on a point system, as if you'll ever land one. My dad paid for a bucket of rings and put them in front of me. A significant investment in my projected success. I put the ring in my mouth and spat it out as I threw my body over the railing. The carny laughed. He took sick pleasure in watching the ring shoot out of my mouth, only to skip along the front bottles. I was hoping this would be an underdog story about how I won against all odds.[58]

The Bat: a rollercoaster that starts forward and then repeats backward. My second favourite ride in the park.

I ran toward it before realizing that I was the only one running now. My team was fading, but I couldn't stop. For the first time since the stunt began, I'd forgotten about the pain and frustration. Maybe, just maybe, I was having fun. The adrenaline was so powerful it drowned out the rest. We approached the ride entrance, expecting to be stopped. And we were.

"I don't think you can get on the ride with that."

"We've gotten this a lot today. We talked with Sarah and she said it was fine."

"Oh, okay then. I just wanted to make sure."

We were shown to our seats and strapped in. This time it was just me, Michael, and Jasmine. Scott and my dad were finished. I could tell Jasmine was having second thoughts, but it was too late. Once those bars go down, there's no turning back.

---

58 It wasn't.

As luck would have it, the ride attendants switched shifts before our launch. A new woman came on deck for a quick once over. Something caught her eye. Me. She came over to reason with a very impatient boy.

"Excuse me sir, but you'll need to step off the ride. You can't hold on."

"Oh, we spoke to the woman before. We have permission from Sarah at head of security." I wasn't worried.

"Do you have a note?" A note? Am I missing gym class? Does it need to be signed by my parents?

"No … but we have footage of the encounter. We've been stopped a lot today, so we spoke about it with her."

"Well, it doesn't really matter if you spoke with the head of security. This is a safety concern. You can't ride like that."

I guess Sarah didn't exactly say I could ride *everything*.

"Look, don't give us a hard time. We've been getting this all day; we paid our money. We don't need this continued harassment. I want to ride with my friends. I want you to leave us alone."

I tried to hide the shock I was experiencing as this garbage was exiting my mouth. It was my first diva moment. Okay, not my first, but it was … one. I wasn't moving.

"Sir, I am the operator of this ride, and I'm instructing you to get off."

Passenger: *"Hey dude, just get off."*

Jasmine: *"We're not getting off."*

Me: *"No. We paid. We have proof that we're allowed. Now start the ride. Please."*

Passengers: *"Get off the ride!"*

Michael: *"Guys—"*

Jasmine and me: *"No."*

Passengers and ride attendants: *"GET OFF!"*

Jasmine and me: *"NO!"*

We got off. It hurt more than the shoulder pain, but I wasn't going down without a fight. I yelled to Scott, *"Get the camera! Show the ride operator!"* He ran over. I wasn't happy and I didn't care who knew it. People began recording me as I lost control.

"*I'll get off your ride, but I will not get off this platform! Don't treat me like I'm nothing because I'm wearing something that frightens you. I told you that I paid, and that I have permission, and that I want to get back on. Look, everyone! I'm going to stand right here until they let us back on the ride! So, you better tell them to get their shit together!*" Guess I had already forgotten my humbling moment from earlier.

Ride attendant: "*Will you please step over here while the ride starts?*"

She put us in a penalty box with a chain. I could see Scott bringing a camera over to the operation booth. I knew it wasn't enough. Now no one in line was a fan of ours. I forgot the whole point of this project. This was supposed to inspire positivity and *not be about me*.

The attendant told us that the head ride operator was on his way. Why did this place have so many heads of everything? I shouted that I was getting on the next ride no matter what. Jasmine pawed me to shut up as I continued lamenting about the unfairness. Michael wasn't saying anything. I noticed Scott across the track with the head ride operator, motioning for me to lower my voice. I did. My anger slowly morphed into embarrassment.

The ride operator signalled us over and we began to explain the situation, albeit a bit frantically. She told us she understood, but that we would have to exit the ride area for the time being. We did. Following us out, she explained that certain attractions had regulations stating that you couldn't ride without the ability to hold on. She told us she would make a list of everything I could ride. Finally, someone was cooperating. I knew, even in the moment, that I'd been an ass. I began backpedalling. Obviously, my mood swings were getting worse because I already couldn't remember why I'd been yelling. I took a minute to breathe while the ride operator made her phone call. We probably wouldn't be able to ride Leviathan, but we might get something great. She came back.

"*I'll be honest, it's only five rides, and they're not the greatest.*"

The list included Chopper Chase, Boo Blasters, and Snoopy's Revolution. If you can't tell by the names, they were all in Kidzville. If you can't tell by that name, this is the children's area of the park.

She left and we were introduced to our new park-assigned-escort-babysitter. She asked us how many of the rides I planned to visit. I told her I would never make it through the whole list,[59] but that there were two I definitely had to check out.

Boo Blasters: a ride where you shoot ghosts on your way through a haunted house. How was this one of the rides you didn't need hands for? You had to hold a gun and fire it. Our escort allowed us to skip the ten-person line. Yippee.[60] I sat down and she put the gun in my lap. Thanks![61] The little cart took off down the track as children began laughing at me. I watched as little ghosts jumped out of the wall and couldn't help but feel lonely. My friends played and laughed and shot at them. Why was such a despondent feeling washing over me? I remember chugging along the little track, arms crossed in front of me, wondering what it all meant.

It was nine p.m. We had a quick dinner and called it a day. But there was one last thing my dad wanted to do before we left.

We made our way to a caricature artist, and he paid for a full body portrait. The man began drawing as I began to fall asleep. All I could feel was a throbbing in my shoulder and sweat dripping off my hands. Another crowd was forming for a good look at me. A woman told me she and her husband had been following me on TV. The husband came over

---

59 This right here, is sarcasm.

60 Sarcasm again.

61 See above.

and started massaging my shoulders as the artist drew me. It was quite an intimate moment to share with a stranger. I actually recommend more people do this for sore-looking people. Give them a back massage (please ask them first). Tell them Mark sent you. The drawing-massage combo finished, and both were equally impressive.

It was time to pack it in. Security was at the gate to say goodbye. Scott wasn't coming home with us, so it was time for us to say goodbye, too. He wished me luck and we arranged to meet again. It was odd. People could drift in and out of this little story and I had to continue living it. I was pretty sad that this day was ending. In between screaming fits, I felt more like myself than I had in days.

I was worried that I would change. Of course, this experience would change me, but what if it wasn't for the best? Could I hang up Jacket Mark when the stunt was over? The ride home was quiet. Some of us slept. The buckles digging into my back kept me up, but I stayed quiet. I didn't feel like complaining anymore.

My dad dropped Michael off at the train station and took Jasmine and me home to Mom's house. He gave me a hug and drove off. My dad is always bragging about me. Growing up, I'd question the sincerity of his public compliments—whether they were genuine, or simply used to further his own image. I used to wonder how often he was *actually* proud. Today I think he was.

Jasmine and I looked at each other in the doorway. She held me so tightly, I couldn't leave. It felt like she was holding me in case I ever tried to. I'd never wanted anything more than to hug her back.

We went downstairs, cleaned my hands, collapsed onto the bed, and shared some moments of tenderness. Jason came over around midnight to hear all about Wonderland. Then, before bed, we got a tweet from Ben Mulroney:

"How's it going @Mark_Correia? Still think this was a good idea? #bathroomblues @etalkCTV"

I didn't.

Jasmine and I worked through a gruelling footage review session. I could barely think about Wonderland, so I suggested we all lie down and finish the conversation in bed. That plan backfired miserably. They were asleep in seconds. I slowly began to fade away, but before I did, a smile crept over my face. The house was completely silent, and I was tied up in the dark, grinning.

DAY 6 – BOWLING SHOES MAKE IT EASIER TO MOONWALK

© Personal Collection

(Nightly Ritual: Going through footage on a 2011 MacBook Pro—2014)

JULY 13, 2014: I came down hard from Wonderland's high. I began taking in what my body was telling me: I was getting sick. The best course of action was to attempt simpler tasks.

Looking back on the footage from day six, it's clear that something is very wrong with me. Most of what I say doesn't make a lick of sense, even more than usual, and the nerves I'm suppressing on camera are coming dangerously close to the surface. It was clear I had been barking at my friends moments before they hit record. There's one clip (I didn't know was being recorded) where I'm pacing back and forth, looking at the ground, before suddenly snapping at Jasmine for standing in the wrong spot. I'm not yelling, just articulating my point aggressively. When I rewatch these moments, I see someone else in my skin. Knowing I'm to blame makes them harder to watch. Harder still, I imagine, to be an unpaid intern/kind-of-girlfriend putting up with it.

It was Max's job to make sure none of those lapses made it into the videos, but that doesn't mean they don't exist. The jacket altered my character in a way I wasn't prepared for, and I wanted the videos to be lighthearted, not to reveal that I was losing it. Still, I was most definitely losing it.

A lot of the footage for that day was useless due to my being half asleep, or fully asleep. There was one fan suggestion that I was dying to record, but my family and friends were against it. Actually, I had been dying to try it *because* my family and friends were against it. Shaving. Someone wanted to see me operate a razor blade without my arms and I was all for it.

I managed to squeeze out some shaving cream, getting most of it in my face and mouth, before putting my electric razor on the edge of the sink. I turned it on and shoved my face into it. The razor ran for about ten seconds in total, and I shaved a little patch into my cheek. Good enough.

I've already revealed the secrets to the bathroom, but a visual clue actually lies hidden in this section of the day six video. I promised myself I wouldn't give too much away, but it's all there.

That afternoon, I went and got a Big Mac as a shout out to McDonald's (one of our corporate sponsors). I ordered the burger and put it in front of me. I planned for an outlandish shot of burger juice and nondescript sauce exploding all over me, ruining the jacket. Only this wasn't the case. It was surprisingly easy. I sort of just sat there and ate it. I don't know why I'm even writing about it. Do I get a paid every time I write the word McDonald's? McDonald's.[62]

Jasmine and Jason helped me through the exhausting moments. That's one thing I really miss. There was something special about waking up with them every morning. I don't know if I can describe how tangible the feeling of love was in that house, but I think it shines through in some of the footage. We just threw some pillows and blankets down, slept when we needed, and did it all again the next day. For each other. For the benefit of others.

Every good magic trick has a secret behind it. The secret behind Escaping Parkinson's was love. I know I keep saying it, but it's super important! It was the people behind the camera stealing kisses or laughs between takes. We didn't meet up every night and drink like any of the other teenagers at that time, we went through footage until our fingers were sore (I know mine were). That's how we made our difference.

Sometimes, when I wasn't working with Jason, he would answer emails in another room to give Jasmine and me space. I took the opportunity

---

62 Please make the cheque out to cash.

to apologize for how I'd been behaving. Neither of them ever held it against me.

Our day of "rest" was cut short by a spontaneous trip to the bowling alley. Mom of course drove us. We got our shoes and made our way over to the lane. Jasmine suggested we use bumpers, so that I had a fighting chance, but I told her that would be cheating. I wasn't taking this jacket off, and I wasn't using no goddamn bumpers. I just liked wearing the shoes. That's why I was there. I'll wear anything that makes physical comedy easier. Better yet, walking on the actual lane. It's greasier than a John Travolta movie.[63] If you walk out onto the lane, you're going to end up on your ass, but you knew that already. It also makes the moonwalk a cakewalk.

It was up to Jason to dress me, like my mother (I mean dress me like my mother would, not dress me how my mom dresses). He put my shoes on and I made the *"Jason was hired solely to put my shoes on"* joke again, which was followed by Jason smacking me in the face with the aforementioned shoe. Well deserved.

Jasmine suggested replacing our names on the screen with: *"Escaping,"* *"Parkinson's,"* and *".com"*, fashioning our own free advertisement. So, we did. Now the twelve other people in the alley would be *so* impressed.

At Wonderland, people were recognizing me left and right. Today, not so much. It'd been a couple days since my last interview, and the novelty was probably wearing off. We got the occasional look, but then everyone looks at teenagers acting like idiots in bowling alleys. To be honest, if it was day one, I would've been disappointed. On day six, I didn't really

---

63 Sorry for this joke. My editor asked me if I wanted to keep it or lose it and I said, *"Ah, keep it."* I regret it deeply.

care. My ball was becoming close friends with the gutter. It had no inter-est in the pins, no matter how hard I kicked it. When Jasmine wasn't positioning my ball for me, she was throwing strikes. Things were getting desperate. I figured smacking my face into the ball might be more effec-tive than using my feet. I was wrong. This time, the ball didn't even make it to the pins. It was cozy in the middle of the gutter, stuck.

Nothing came down to reset the round, nothing happened at all, until a very unimpressed lane attendant came over. He kicked the ball into the return and made sure to tell us that half of our time was up.

I pushed the ball to the line and set it up just where I wanted it. I kicked it hard. It spun straight down the middle, connecting between the first and second pin. Wait, could it be? I crouched down. They all toppled over, leaving one pin rocking back and forth. It fell. A strike! I jumped up and down screaming at Jason, who was screaming back at me. Jasmine was filming with a smirk.

My legs buckled and Jason brought me to a chair. It was time to go.

I fell asleep on the way home, and woke up in the basement with Jasmine and Jason on either side of me. It was already over? The day had shot by.

Jason popped in the footage and we worked slowly, Jasmine continu-ally shaking me awake. I kept opening my eyes to her worried face. Why was she worried? Where was I?

"Hey, can we call it quits?" We could send the footage in the morning, right?

I remember Jasmine blowing hand sanitizer into my hands and tucking me in. *"You have a big interview tomorrow morning."*

I did?

DAY 7 - DON'T ASK ABOUT MY BANJO

© Personal Collection

(You Never Forget: Riding a bike—2014)

JULY 14, 2015: Out of bed, I floated. I wandered the basement all morning, staring at the couch, entranced by the patterns. No longer in touch with what emotion I was feeling. Every contraption in the house was falling apart with its creator. I'd bitten the tape off the doorknobs, the hooks were snapping off the walls, and my toothbrush was peeling from the sink. I looked in the mirror to see a brush hanging from my giggling mouth.

Foggy.

Mom was waiting outside. Why? Oh, we had an important appointment. Right. An interview on a popular radio show. I was flying solo, because Jason and Jas had previous engagements. What were they? No clue.

The traffic was worse than usual. I remember that. We weren't getting to Toronto for a while. My mom tuned in to a traffic report. A tractor trailer had rolled over on the highway. I wasn't worried. I was catatonic.

We arrived fifteen minutes behind schedule, and so I ran up to the studio as fast as I could. They were on the air. The host made a little gesture with his hand to come sit down. I sat between him and his co-host. We were airing later now, which was a better slot anyway.

"Up next: Mark Correia is a world-renowned magician, and he's currently doing a fundraiser for Michael J. Fox."

World-renowned? I'll take it. And soon after: *"Welcome back. Now, the magician who put himself in a straitjacket to raise funds for Parkinson's research. Mark?"*

I was fighting through a thick fog, but I think I was talking about my passion, and that definitely gave me some much-needed strength. We spoke about the stunt, where listeners could donate, and of my love for Michael J. Fox. I was sure to sing my team's praises when I could.

I then christened the radio waves with never-before-uttered bathroom talk, absentmindedly adding: *"My friends help sometimes."*

The co-host had a question on his mind. You could see him stewing over something. Waiting to pounce. When the conversation broke, he shifted in his chair and asked. *"So how do you ... um, strum your banjo?"*

Before I could reply, the main host swallowed and changed the subject. I didn't speak, move, or blink. They shared the links to the cause and closed the show.

When we stepped away from the microphones, I realized that I had been given twenty minutes of airtime. A very generous gesture. They both asked if they could sign the jacket and I told them I'd be honoured.

My mom drove me back to Oakville as we listened to the show. Everything sounded great, I think. Then Jasmine called and told me that we were walking over to Jason's later to play video games. Someone had suggested it. I remember the heat. Sweating into my own eyes, feeling giggly as I hobbled down the hot sidewalk. Mood still swinging.[64] The walk to Jason's house was long enough for me to deliver a rambling monologue about the importance of our stunt to a stunned Jasmine.

Burnt out, I sat down with Jason. Sleep was what I needed. Video games were what we'd promised our viewers.

Jason chose *Halo*, because that's what the teens were down with back then. He set up a controller at my feet and we started playing. I was expected to run around, switch weapons, aim at my opponent, and fire. I was using one toe to run around and the other toe to aim. What I thought would just raise my frustration actually turned out to be pretty fun! Jason wasn't going easy on me though. He was killing me.[65] Every time. Obviously. Jasmine was howling with laughter. We repeated this about ten times for the camera. Not because we needed the shot, but because that's just what was happening.

---

64 Post stunt I would find out that I was suffering from some serious dehydration.

65 In the game.

After lots of trial and error, I somehow managed to position my character around a corner, aim my weapon, and kill Jason not once, but twice.[66] I decided to quit while I was ahead. I was also challenged to walk a dog. Jasmine clipped up Jason's dog, Macy, and we all went outside. My first instinct was to use my mouth, but I realized my teeth had probably been through enough abuse. If Macy decided to take off, I was probably going to lose a canine.[67] I put the leash around my neck instead. Smart! It tightened the more Macy moved, but it was funny, so fuck it.

I feel like I should mention that I'm not suggesting you hurt yourself on a daily basis for the purpose of entertaining others. However, Andy Kaufman once said that *"if one person is smiling, then I've done my job."*[68]

We'd completed our tasks and it was now time to talk media. We still hadn't secured Toronto's most popular morning show, *Breakfast Television*. We'd sent them emails, gone there in person, and still nothing. Time for the guerrilla tactics which had been working so far. We had to wake up at five a.m. to attempt a walk on.

---

66 In the game.

67 This is the funniest joke in the book by the way, so if you don't like it, put it down now.

68 Okay, after looking for the exact wording of this quote, I've come to realize that Andy Kaufman never said it. Actually, I can't find any comedian who ever said it. I've been living my life based off an Andy Kaufman quote that doesn't exist. He would probably love that.

It was nearing the time where I'd steal Jason and Jasmine from their parents and bring them to my house to keep an eye on me.[69]

I'd gone seven days without a shower, and I needed to bathe *somehow*. It was frightening how itchy everything below the belt had become. You can't go two weeks without washing and expect not to get an infection. Let that be a lesson to you, kids.

The only way I could get clean was with Jasmine's help. I stepped out of one pant leg, and we pulled the pants through the crotch strap to reveal my naked … banjo. Then, Jasmine put a garbage bag over me and my shell, tucking it into the bottom of the jacket so it wouldn't get wet. I walked to my bedroom and listened to Jasmine fill the tub.

The loss of independence in that moment was gut wrenching. Sorry this isn't the softcore erotica you were hoping for. I slumped down onto the bed, buried my face in the sheets, and cried. Jasmine gave me the space I needed. I heard the tub stop and watched as the bathroom light projected her shadow onto me. She was waiting. I rolled over as best I could. She came to me and sat on the edge of the bed. With a soft hand, she wiped away the tears I couldn't reach. I wondered if she felt like she was in the jacket, too. In many ways, she was. She was with me the whole time.

She eased me into the warm water. The crotch strap soaked completely. She lathered me softly and took the time to scratch my itches. I was completely helpless, but she made me feel safe. Her generosity was overwhelming. I wondered if I could ever find that again in someone else. After the bath, she slowly dried me off, put my pants back on, and tousled my hair.

---

69 Let that sink in. Jasmine and Jason forfeited a full two weeks of their summer in order to watch me sleep.

DAY 8 - A COOL-HEADED PROTAGONIST NO LONGER

© Personal Collection

(Exhaustion: Fast asleep on the train—2014)

TWO WEEKS STRAIT
HOW TO SUCCEED WHEN YOUR HANDS ARE TIED

5:OO A.M. ON JULY 15, 2014: Something about the way even *I* wasn't enjoying my own company told me that today wasn't going to be a good one. My dad was at the front door before I'd fully articulated my funk. Ever since I was a cute little kid, my father would point at the various guests on *Breakfast Television* and say, *"That's gonna be you someday."* Today, that kid was a grumpy teenager who hadn't slept. I got out of bed barking at Jasmine and Jason. New territory.

Being in a straitjacket for two weeks is like hanging from monkey bars and waiting for your arms to go numb. They do eventually, but not without torturing you with waves of pain (before you inevitably let go). Well, I couldn't let go. And today the pain was surging.

I kept my distance from Jasmine. Usually my impulses are a great thing,[70] but today I was tense and rude, so the best course of action was to separate myself.

After Jason made waffles, we had fifteen minutes to get ready. I rushed upstairs with Jasmine to brush my teeth. Since the toothbrush was no longer attached to the sink, she held it for me. She tried to brighten my morning, but I found her irritating.

On day eight, I snapped. If there was ever a time where I should've called off the stunt and screamed *"Dakota"* at the top of my lungs, it was then, in the upstairs bathroom, fifteen minutes before we had to get out of the house. Jasmine was trying to help me. That's all she ever tried to do. I know this now. I was expecting the jacket to constrict me physically; I was prepared for that. The real challenge spawned from my need for control, my difficulty in asking for help, and the assumption that my emotions were not my responsibility. My coping mechanism, which once consisted of spending time alone, was no longer available to me. Instead of finding constructive releases, I became a pot of water on the stove:

---

70 For comedy.

simmering while being watched, overflowing the second cameras weren't rolling. I became someone unrecognizable to myself.

I've thought a lot about skipping this section of the story. This is my book; I can write myself as the cool-headed protagonist with an overwhelmingly kind heart if I want to. I could, but I won't. In writing and rewriting, I've had to address underlying issues in my past, especially concerning my relationships. I allowed myself to speak to Jasmine in disrespectful ways while demanding better work, because I saw her as my helper. I didn't speak to Jason in the same way. That is damaging, sexist behaviour. Jasmine and I had a blowup in the bathroom. A big argument. With shouting and blaming and crying. I won't go into the minute details because I want to respect her privacy and don't feel it would be fair to hash out *my* side of a private encounter in *my* book. I know she would not appreciate my retelling it at this moment in time. She may even see my apology as an attempt to quell my own guilt ... But I'm going to apologize anyway. What happened in that white-tiled, bathroom-cage was *my fault.* After days of snarky comments and contempt, I went wayward. I crossed a line. I'm sorry. After our fight, I stormed out and waited for her to come back to me. Manipulative, I know. Eventually, I went in and apologized. *"I'm sorry, you're right."*

Too little too late. *"I don't know what else to do, Mark. We'll talk later."*

Did the jacket have influence over my decision-making and state of being? You bet your ass. But you can also bet your ass that it was no excuse to act like a prick.

When we arrived at the station, I took Jasmine aside and said, *"After the stunt is over, I want you to forget about me."*

See, sometimes when I fuck up, instead of actually focusing on the other person, I just double down on the self-loathing. It's a nasty habit.

"Don't be so dramatic," she said.

It was around six a.m. We had an hour before they started taping. Everyone was still arriving. We watched as crew came in and out. Me, my friends, and my father stood outside in the morning rain. Waiting.

Jason tweeted one of the anchors, but it was clear by her reply that she had no control over programming. She tweeted back, saying, *"Good luck."*

I looked over to check in with Jasmine, and she mouthed: *"It's fine."* Is it?

Finally, a man came outside to check on us.

"Hi, I'm Mark Correia—blah blah blah—stunt—blah blah blah—strait-jacket—blah blah blah—Michael J. Fox—blah blah blah—Parkinson's research. Could I please speak with the segment producer?"

"Yeah sure, I'll grab him—blah blah blah—today's already planned—blah blah blah—squeeze you in."

He went back inside, and my dad went to buy an umbrella before telling me that he was dying for a coffee. I think we all were.

After a while, the segment producer came down.

"Hey guys, I've been getting your emails. We really appreciate what you're doing—" yeah, yeah, this work is really valuable, but? *"But we can't have you on because of* Breakfast TV *policy. You've already appeared on* The Morning Show, *and we don't compete with other networks. This is our policy with everything that comes through Toronto. Even celebrity interviews."*

I thought that sounded like the shittiest policy on earth, but what I said was: *"We completely understand, and we'd love to appear on the show with future projects."*

I was disappointed. I know my dad was too. Pretty soon, I had another plan: Walk behind the back window while they were filming. But today, the show was being shot upstairs. Damn. All this for nothing.

"I'm going to go get some coffee," my dad said. *"What do you guys want?"*

He left with our orders, and we walked around the square. Dejected.

With a *"C'mere"* tilt of her head, Jasmine pulled me aside. I could tell by her shifting stance that she'd been mulling over her thoughts since our last encounter. I had too. But that's an understatement. My mind became a film reel playing the greatest hits of our relationship: our first kiss, our first date, our first dinner with parents. I remembered who she was before our bad habits. The way her cheeks would flush when I surprised her, how her laugh was almost a squeak, the way she said *"I love you."*

I have this tendency to mourn before death in an attempt to forewarn my heart. The line had blurred between fighting *for* Jasmine and fighting *with* Jasmine. Fighting is only valuable if all parties are fighting *toward* something. If Jasmine had left me right there, I would have let her go. So, I straightened my confined back, and prepared for her to make the transition from my present to my past.

"Look," she spoke purposefully, *"I know you're not yourself. But I will not be treated that way. Okay?"*

Another chance. I had to stop myself from instantly agreeing, jumping to any sense of security. I took a moment, and I answered.

"Never again."

When Jasmine hugged me, I engraved the feeling of her touch in my memory. I promised myself I'd never take her for granted again. *"Never again,"* I whispered into her shoulder.

A man approached us and asked for change. He needed some breakfast. I told Jason to give him the five in my wallet.

"Thanks man!" he said. *"I'll have to wait until something opens up now."* We told him that we were doing the same thing.

"Well, best of luck to you, I'll see you around." He didn't ask about the jacket.

Before we got back in the car, I had an idea. I took my friends to the middle of an empty Dundas Square and looked at the big screen I'd been on six days ago. I could see little versions of us in the background of the *Breakfast Television* broadcast. We jumped, ran back and forth, and made a big scene. Not exactly what I'd hoped for. But when we walked out of frame, we knew we'd accomplished our goal in some way. We were *technically* on *Breakfast Television*.[71]

We had a dilemma on our hands (or lack thereof). We didn't have time to travel home to Oakville and then back downtown before our next meeting, and we didn't want to stand outside for three hours. My dad drove us to a mall so we could kill some time. We made our way over to the massage chairs and wasted a few coins. If you've ever used a mall massage chair, you'll know why I say waste. But if you've ever spent two weeks in a straitjacket, you'll know why I settled.[72]

My anger eventually flattened into depression. I was done faking good moods. We moved from the chairs where we'd been for over an hour and sat on a mall bench. Jason turned on the camera and I gave an honest confessional. How am I feeling, folks? Helpless.

Jasmine and Jason wanted snacks. I told them to go ahead as I sunk deeper into the bench. They returned with beaming smiles on their faces.

"Something to cheer you up." They handed me a cola bottle that said: *"Mark."* It worked. They had *"Jas"* and *"Jay"* bottles for themselves. I've tried to convince this company to turn the footage into a commercial, but I guess the straitjacket community isn't their market. They are mine, though (I see you reading this with your feet).

As we began collecting our things, a security guard approached us.

Security guard: *"So, what're you doing here at the mall?"*

Jasmine: *"Sitting."*

Security guard: *"What's with the straitjacket?"*

Me: *"We're doing a fundraising event for—"*

Security guard: *"Yes, I saw one of your cards, you're the Terry Fox people."*

---

71 I've since been on for real. Dad was proud.

72 Actually, if you've ever done that, you should contact me and I'll show you how to milk it into a book deal.

Me: *"Actually, we're raising money for the Michael J. Fox Foundation."*

Security guard: *"He have cancer?"*

Me: *"No. Parkinson's."*

Security guard: *"Oh."* Pause. *"I'm sorry, but we can't have you guys in the mall."*

An argument! Just what I was looking for.

Me: *"Why can't we be in the mall?"*

Security guard: *"Because you're going to alarm one of our guests."*

Me: *"Why?"*

I motioned at Jason to start shooting. As soon as the red light came on, he became more reasonable.

Security guard: *"Okay, okay, it's fine. Just don't stay for too long."*

Me: *"We were on our way out, actually."*

We packed up our stuff and headed toward the subway. It was my first time riding in the jacket. Believe me, you see much stranger things on the train. I hardly got any looks.

The sun was shining, but it wasn't hot, which meant that we could walk to our next appointment. Our story was being picked up by The Canadian Press (TCP).

TCP is a media outlet that larger networks pull stories from. Most networks don't have time to cover every story personally, and this is where TCP comes in. They do a write-up and video as a package for other networks. It can change everything, really. It's the difference between one newspaper and hundreds.

As we walked down King Street toward TCP, we happened upon the headquarters of the *Toronto Sun*. The *Sun* was a paper I read as a kid. The comics, anyway. Walking into main offices now had a fifty percent success rate, so I decided to try one more time. The stunt sounds great on paper, but you don't get the full effect until a guy in a straitjacket walks into your workplace. Before entering, we were stopped by a woman screaming about a chemical spill. She was going on about catching the first plane out of Canada. I tried talking to her.

"Excuse me, is everything alright?"

"Don't drink the water! The newspapers aren't running my stories!"

I told her that I was about to go upstairs, and I would ask about it. She calmed down and walked away.

"Hi! My name is Mark Correia, and I have a story about ..." etc., etc.

"Let me call someone down to speak with you."

A woman entered the lobby and asked if we had a notepad. We did.

"Here are the people to email directly if you want your story run." I almost had time to thank her before she began spouting the emails.

"Is that all you need?" she asked.

"Um. Could we just come up now?"

Her face twisted into a smile. *"Maybe you'll have better luck somewhere else."* She turned to go.

"Oh, one more thing!" I said. She turned around. *"Is there a chemical spill I should know about?"*

She looked puzzled. *"Not that I know of."*

"Oh. Well, if there is, could you run that story?"

She paused. *"Sure."* Then, she turned and went upstairs. The secretary was smiling as we walked away.

"You guys should try Sun TV News."

I turned around. *"Huh?"*

"Sun TV News," he said. *"Your story looks better on TV. I saw you guys on Citytv."*

"Where is it?"

He pointed out the door. *"Right across the street."*

There was an alarm sounding in the *Sun TV News* building as we entered. Was that for us? I wasn't in the mood to meet more security. We saw a woman pacing the lobby, screaming about a chemical spill.[73] It looked like she was finally getting some attention. I walked up to the front desk and began my pitch.

Me: *"Hi! My name is Mark Correia, and I ..."* etc., etc.

Woman: *"Sir, this isn't really a good time. We're in the middle of a security breach."* Wow, this tactic really wasn't working today.

Me: *"Security breach?"*

Woman (frowning): *"Yes. It appears as though a crazy woman has wandered into our lobby."*

Me: *"To be fair, I'm wearing a straitjacket ..."*

(Pause)

Me: *"... For Parkinson's Research."*

(Pause)

Me: *"Michael J. Fox."*

Woman: *"Okay, give me your info. We'll get in touch later."*

Me (whispering to Jason): *"That's a no."*

She took out a little sticky note and wrote down all the information for the segment producers.

Woman: *"Sorry, it just isn't a good time."*

Me: *"Not if we can't drink the water, no."*

We stopped at a cafe on the way to TCP. The following played out like a sitcom: Spoons clinking on mugs. Coffee shop chatter. The bell on the door jingled as I tore in ... the cafe went silent. I stood still and waited for the chatter to pick up. It eventually did, but everyone's eyes stayed on me.

Jasmine took me to the bathroom[74] and Jason ordered some coffee. The only thing I hated more than pooping was pooping outside the house.

---

73 The same woman. There weren't two.

74 It's worth noting how quickly Jasmine jumped back into taking care of me after I had treated her so poorly that same morning.

I didn't have my usual tools, so it made everything more … interesting. After about twenty minutes, I emerged from the singular men's washroom with a girl in tow. People were, rightfully, still staring.

I sat down to my coffee before being tapped on the shoulder.

"I knew it was you! I saw you on The Morning Show!"

Now people were wondering who I was. Jasmine took the opportunity to give everyone a card to remember us by.

"We're here for The Canadian Press." I spoke into an intercom as Jason held the button.

The doors opened to reveal an extravagant lobby. A reporter welcomed us into the office. People began whispering. I guess I still had that effect. This was one of the rare interviews where my stress got the best of me. When asked if I would ever attempt this again, I said, without missing a beat, *"No! God no! I was just saying I would never do something like this again. I knew it would hurt physically, but the psychological aspect is too much. We take our hands for granted."*

07.16.14

Hello Mark,

This is Paul from Sun TV News.

I love your story and we'd like to have you on 'Straight Talk' at around 4:30. Could you email us back ASAP to confirm?

- Paul

Sun TV News

We'd done it again. This time with nothing more than a security breach and a sticky note.

Keeping media interested in a story for two weeks is a tough task. Yet, here we were, in the *Sun TV News* lobby on day eight. I met the host, gave him some background information, and we were live.

Probably my favourite interview. The more jokes the anchor cracked, the more I opened up. Our segment ran at five o'clock. Another prime time spot. We thanked everyone in the studio, and they all replied, *"Come back soon!"*[75]

Our appointments were finished, which meant making our way to Union Station and catching the train home. An old friend was waiting for us at the entrance. The man we'd met outside of *Breakfast Television* and given a few dollars to ten hours earlier. He recognized us immediately.

"Hey guys! How are you doing?"

We spoke briefly. Even after a full conversation, he didn't ask why I was wearing the jacket. He was the *only person* throughout the whole stunt that didn't bring it up. I loved that.

Jason told him that we were going to McDonald's and asked if he wanted anything.

"Two junior chickens and a cola would be awesome."

The long line was the only thing between us and those burgers. We were all hungry, some more than others.

We got our bags and delivered one outside. The man thanked us, and I said, *"Thank McDonald's."* We smiled and ran to catch our train.

Jasmine held my arm and stuffed a Big Mac in my mouth. It was one of the best—okay, I'm getting the feeling that this whole book sounds like one big fucking commercial. Let me just say, neither McDonald's nor the nondescript cola company are sponsoring any of this book in any way shape or form.[76]

---

75 *Sun TV* is now out of business. I don't think it had to do with our visit.

76 No matter how many emails I write them …

Jasmine and Jason shook me awake. It was our stop. They escorted me to my mom's car. Jasmine passionately reiterated the day's events to my mom. I relaxed as she recounted the best parts of the worst day thus far. Maybe this relationship would survive after all.

Jasmine's retelling was interrupted by the ping of her phone. Her eyes widened as she checked her email. She had an interview to be the lead makeup artist on a popular web series. We tried to contain our excitement, but Jason ended up screaming. She was happy, so we were too.

"I know I won't get it, but it's nice to be recognized." Good practice for her first Oscar nomination.

The interview was the next morning, meaning Jasmine would leave us early. She offered to stay around if we needed help.

"Are you kidding?" I said. *"Go be famous!"* She gave me a little smile. Today had certainly been the hump of the stunt; nine p.m. and we were all in bed. I turned to say something to Jasmine, but she was already asleep. And then, so was I.

DAY 9 - SMELL ME

© Personal Collection
(Jason D'Souza)

(My Hero: Some guy in a costume picks me up—2014)

TWO WEEKS STRAIT
HOW TO SUCCEED WHEN YOUR HANDS ARE TIED

JULY 16, 2014: Truthfully, I don't remember day nine. I'm sure it happened, but I didn't live it. I have hazy memories of breakfast. I don't really remember Jasmine leaving for her interview. But I remember it was just Jason and me.

We'd already filmed most of the harder breakfast requests, so I let myself off the hook and chose cereal ... which ended up being the hardest breakfast. I was done being graceful, and I don't blame myself.

I threw the box up onto the counter with my foot. Shaking the bag out of the box with my teeth, cereal fell "into" the bowl. Simple enough. Then, milk. I hooked the handle of the pitcher on my bottom lip (which hurt), ran over to the bowl, and promptly began spilling it all over the counter. I wasn't bothered by the mess; I was bothered by the fact that I hadn't seen my own hands in nine days.

Jasmine came home in a great mood, just in time to review our Canadian Press story. A quick google of "Escaping Parkinson's" revealed all the papers across North America that were running it. We even had a few overseas. It had been picked up by almost every Toronto newspaper: the *Toronto Star*, the *Globe and Mail*, the *National Post*, you name it, we were in it. Even the *Toronto Sun*, who'd initially rejected our story. Go figure.[77]

I tried juggling as one suggestion. Turns out, not actually possible at all. Jasmine and Jason decided to pick up the slack. It only takes one throw to get hooked on juggling. As you refuse to admit defeat, you become more frustrated. *"Holy shit, this is hard."* I could see the determination glimmering in Jason's eyes. Juggling had claimed another victim. I coached them as best as I could. It was a relief to focus on something new. It may seem innocent, but juggling is a gateway drug. An interest in juggling can quickly become an interest in magic.

---

77 No news about that chemical spill though.

For those of you who picked up this book in a magic bookstore (magic, not magical … though if you do happen to find a magical bookstore, please send me the address), you may be looking for practical how-tos. You would've quickly found out that this is not a tutorial book, unless you want to know how to spend two weeks in a straitjacket, and again, I don't condone that. But I'd like to think my writing will inspire people to take an interest in magic. For now, let's start with juggling. I'll explain it to you as I explained it to Jason and Jasmine, with much difficulty. If you're physically able, I ask you to procure three objects of roughly the same size. Spheres work best for beginners. Throw them into the air, one at a time. Now, here's the most important part: catch them. And now, you're juggling!

If you've been reading and juggling simultaneously, congratulations! If you're like Jasmine and Jason, you're not! We decided to learn from watching. I showed them videos of my favourite jugglers and magicians. We were actually taking a break.

I have posters in my basement of Kellar, Houdini, and Thurston. Jason asked what each one was known for. We spent hours discussing magic history, and he spent hours trying to work out the secrets. I would always say, *"Interesting. You're close."* He never was, but I saw his eyes opening to things he'd never considered. Something was changing in him, slowly. I wasn't sure what, but art has a nasty way of doing that. I think we became best friends that day.

A call from Marion was always a good thing.

"Are you okay to meet with CBC later?"

I thought for a moment. *"Fuck yes."*

CBC is the primary network in Canada. It's our NBC. We scrambled to get the house ready before the reporter arrived. When she did arrive, she told me she'd never interviewed someone in a straitjacket before, which was hard to believe.

First, we shot an unusually long interview, which gave me the chance to really open up. Then, she told me she'd forgot to wire me for sound. Great. Apparently, the scratch audio on the camera was good enough, so we kept moving. She then interviewed Jasmine and Jason. Their faces lit up. It was nice to see them talk about why this was important to *them*, the awareness they wanted to raise, and why they had gotten involved. She remembered to mic both of them as an added bonus.

After a shot of Jason spraying Febreze on my hands, the reporter asked, *"Can I smell?"* It was honestly the craziest thing I'd been asked so far.

"Sure, but you don't want to." She put her face right into the sleeve and shot back like lightning, a look of pure terror in her eyes.

"I warned you."

I couldn't possibly relay the smell via literature, but my hands smelled like feet after a soccer game, and hands have no business smelling like feet.

7.16.14

Hi Mark!

I write for the Huffington Post's Impact section and just came across your straitjacket charity mission. I love what you're doing and would like to write a piece about it for HuffPost.

Can you please email me some photos I can include?

Best,

Huffington Post

A popular New York publication was running our story! I was thrilled. Jason quickly emailed back. I did my best to answer the questions coherently, and the reporter told me she would send the article when it was online. This was a pivotal moment.

We went to Jason's house and turned on CBC. I wanted to watch it at his place, so I could see his mom's reaction to him being on TV. She screamed. After the segment ran, we hit eight thousand dollars in donations and I couldn't have been happier. A welcome change from day eight.

Oil and grime were creating a thick film over my skin. Back to my house ... I needed another bath, and by bath, I mean a shampoo and a leg scrub.

I was dreading "bath time" since my last breakdown. Jasmine threaded my head through a hole in a garbage bag as I leaned over the tub in my childhood home. She filled a pitcher with suds and water and poured it over me. I was enveloped in the lukewarm mixture. The droplets that didn't ricochet off my plastic shell traced my face, landing in the pockets of my eyes, nose, and mouth. The towel wrapped around my neck became heavy. Restrained, breathing spurts of water, I felt myself shrink, and then I felt myself softly begin to shake.

I whimpered and whined like a dog, inaudible beneath the pitter-patter of water on plastic. My muscles ached, my lungs burned, and I was being bathed. How profoundly I had lost my independence. I focused my gaze on the bathtub drain as I began to cry. Jasmine and Jason existed in a different world, merely inches above me, unaware. They joked with each other as my tears circled the drain, mixing with the soapy water.

The hurricane lessened to a drizzle as the water turned off. Jasmine patted my face dry with an old towel. Our eyes met. She had always been able to see me in a way that no one else could. She knew when I was lying, on the verge of breaking down, or when I simply needed her. I don't know what she saw in me that night. All I know is that she brought me comfort.

The world around us melted away. Time slowed with my heart rate as she ran her fingers through my hair. She dried her palms on the towel. I closed my eyes and felt warmth spread through me. The pain, emotion, and exhaustion I'd been holding hostage evaporated from my body with one flash of her knowing eyes.

She didn't say I love you. She didn't have to. I don't know if she understood that the message was reciprocated, but that was the beautiful part. She wasn't asking.

As we lay in our beds that night, I let the gravity of the day sink into the mattress. I listened as the breathing and chuckles quieted to a stop, imagining faces in the ceiling's popcorn finish. I was sure the others were asleep when Jason began to softly snore.

I struggled to roll over and was met with blue eyes. Jasmine, looking at me from her perch on the couch. Carefully, so as not to wake Jason, she lifted the blanket and crawled off the couch. She made her way onto my mattress, slipped her arm around me, and buried her face into my chest. The soft scent of her hair, singing me to sleep.

She'd been waiting, too.

DAY 10 - FAT LIP

(Still Got It: Performing a card trick on Morning Live—2014)

JULY 17, 2014: "Four days left." The words fell from my mouth as I creaked into sitting position. The smell of bacon filled my nostrils. I was relieved to discover that Jasmine hadn't killed me in my sleep, as my nightmares had suggested. Instead, she was nuzzled up next to me.

My mom was making breakfast, and Jason was answering fan emails. The jacket was getting old, but none of that was.

First stop: News. *Morning Live.* It was the smallest holding pen yet, but somehow also the greatest. There was a couch guests could sign and lots of donuts. Donuts! I ate three while I waited, and asked someone to wipe my mouth. To tell you the truth, I have no recollection of signing the couch. I know how stupid it would've been not to, but I have a really hard time remembering what happened after the donuts.

"Mr. Correia, you're needed on set."

I was shown where to stand and introduced to the anchor. As I was getting wired up, I noticed a clock counting down. Only three minutes before we were live. And I was supposed to perform a magic trick today! Can you believe it? The anchor helped me put my cards on the table as I continued getting anxious. Sixty seconds to perform a magic trick and get important messages about Parkinson's across.

"And we're live."

Making a short story shorter, the anchor selected the king of clubs from the deck, and I raised my arms to reveal a big predicted king of clubs drawing on the straitjacket. The trick went off without a hitch (somehow).

My mouth began to fail me as garbled sentences poured out of it, but the anchor helped me along. I delivered lame joke after stock line, and he laughed politely. I felt like a drunk, hack comic. Good thing this was my last interview before the live event.

Afterward, my mom helped me into the car and read a text from my dad. All of his friends from Montreal were sending him pictures of my face in the *Montreal Gazette* newspaper. It's funny when people see you in a paper you didn't know you would be featured in. It was reassuring to be represented in my other city, in another language.

And ... that's what I remember! Everything else from this day is a mystery. Certain images are very clear in my head, like driving to Toronto with my mom, but other than that it's a blank. Scott was trying to arrange a trip to the gym to film me using the equipment. That wasn't until midnight. What did we do before that? It's lost in the deep recesses of my memory.

As a seasoned performer, Scott is much wiser than I'll ever be. He strongly believes that if you don't feel up to performing, you don't have to. He kept reminding me that being "on" twenty-four seven could be exhausting. It was sweet of him to remind me, but I had yet to learn this lesson. I felt guilty every time I sat down. Not having my arms made me feel pretty useless as it was, so not entertaining on top of that was nearly impossible. I gave in and tried to relax for a second. Something surprising happened.

Relaxation?

No. Pain. Not the usual soreness and discomfort either. Shooting pain in my arms. It scared me, but I didn't bring it up. I will, however, say that if you, dear reader, experience shooting pains, consult a doctor. Don't be like me.

As soon as I got up to do something, or even engage in conversation about work, the feeling would ease off. Clearly, I was in a lot more pain than I thought, and these activities were merely serving as a distraction. Some adrenaline to keep me going. Something *had* to have kept me going.

Scott could tell that I was restless, so he suggested shooting another suggestion. I remembered one of the funniest requests I had received throughout the stunt, and Scott was the only one who could make it happen. We went to the backyard with his straitjacket and the camera. The task was to wear a straitjacket. Not the one I had on. Another one. Over top of it. He hit record and put his jacket over mine. He crossed the sleeves in front of my arms, buckled them, and reached between my legs. Two crotch straps for the price of one.

"Can you escape from it?" he asked. I looked at him, then back at the second jacket.

"Will you donate to the foundation if I do?" He took me up on the challenge.

"What's the time limit?" he asked. I wasn't keen on any time limit, but after some negotiation, we agreed on five minutes. I can do my regular escape in about a minute and a half, so I figured that would be plenty of time. Right?

First: focus. I let out all my breath to gain slack. Then, I began shaking the sleeves over my head, assisted by my teeth. Now, with the jacket on loosely, I just had to find a way to undo the crotch strap. With time ticking down I panicked and began to drag my ass across a brick wall. I would have been more reckless and probably a little faster, but I didn't want to undo the crotch strap on *my* straitjacket by accident. It would be a shame if I accidentally escaped both of them.

I abandoned this plan and began stepping through the strap to get my leg on the other side. I just about broke my ankle when the strap suddenly snapped free. I looked up, awaiting my results. It took me five minutes and fifteen seconds. Scott looked at me.

"That is one of the most impressive things I have ever seen. I'm still donating."

How's that for a testimonial from a guy who jumps out of planes handcuffed?

When it got dark, Scott drove us to the gym. Immediately, I was reminded that I had no business there. I don't go to the gym, even when I *have* arms. We were filming at midnight, and I was still trying to be a barrel of laughs through my ten-day exhaustion. There were still some people working out, so we didn't get to use all the dangerous stuff, like the treadmill. I was pretty bummed, because I knew that no pain meant no … views.

My second-worst injury throughout the stunt occurred at the gym, and funnily enough, it was before I'd even started to work out. I was trying to tap the "on" button on an elliptical machine with my nose. I pressed it into the screen, but it did nothing. I smashed it again, still nothing. I went at it even harder and must have caught my lip between the edge of the screen and my teeth because boy did it feel like I had caught my lip between the edge of the screen and my teeth. It looks like a harmless tap in the video, but my lip was bruised and purple for the rest of the stunt. Every time I ate, I bit my fat lip, which didn't help the healing process.

Then it was onto the punching bag. I tried kicking it and came straight down onto my kneecap. It isn't hard to notice this one. You hear my knee hit the wood with a loud *crack* in the footage. I now had a clicking knee to match my shoulder.

We cut the workout short because I had no idea what the fuck I was doing, and I was bound to hurt myself (irrevocably).

Scott told me he was taking me out for Indian food with his girl-friend, Alex.

We picked up our friends, Rosemary Reid and Aaron Fisher, along the way.[78] Two amazing magicians who have been even more amazing mentors to me. They're some of my favourite people, and I was happy to spend time with two people who weren't Jasmine and Jason.[79] Scott drove to the restaurant while I twiddled my thumbs.[80] Aaron began congratu-

---

78 Rosemary was my original creative writer all those months ago.

79 But not as happy as Jasmine and Jason.

80 Metaphorically.

lating me on everything so far. I distinctly remember how good that felt coming from him (look him up).

Scott ordered for me and we sat down. I looked at Alex. She felt the pressure, and offered to feed me. *"Please do."* After she fed me my entire meal, Aaron and Rosemary offered to sign the crotch strap. What are friends for, right? Did I mention we were in a restaurant? He made sure to draw a happy face in the "O" of his name. It was in the perfect spot too…

We got back to Scott's around one a.m. It was a long dinner. My mom was there, waiting to receive me. She hated when I was out this late. She was convinced that I would run myself into the ground and get sick. She was, of course, correct.

Jasmine was awaiting my arrival with good news: she'd booked the makeup gig! I was so excited I kissed her … in front of Jason. I hadn't done that in months. He gave me a knowing look. Her first day of production was unfortunately the last day of the stunt. I hugged her as best as I could and we agreed to be there for each other in spirit.

Shortly after, Jason called me about a boat. Not the Jason you know and love, but my (only) other friend, Jason Stephanian. His parents were part of a yacht club in Etobicoke[81] and he was curious to know if I wanted to borrow a sailboat … and sail that boat. My ears perked up, but I was apprehensive. My jacket didn't get along with water. Nor did I without arms. Based on what I knew about sailing boats, it involved a lot of water. But I'm no doctor. I would've been a fool to pass this up. So, I jumped on board.[82]

---

81 Yes, a small town outside Toronto.

82 Pun intended.

Tonight's suggested task was Jason spending it in his own house. It came from Jason's mother. Fair. This gave me and Jasmine a night alone. What we did or spoke about is lost in another part of my mind. These weeks were some of the most profound in my life, and still, so many powerful memories from those fourteen days escape me.

DAY 11 - NO HANDS ON DECK

(I'm the Captain Now: Sailing in a straitjacket—2014)

JULY 18, 2014: I woke up feeling … rested. Which was odd, considering that I'd fallen asleep at three a.m. Wait. It was noon. No one had woken me up. I'd grown used to my friends hustling hours before I was even awake, but now Jasmine was out cold, my mom was asleep upstairs, and Jason was most likely sleeping in his own bed. The stunt was taking its toll on everyone.

Jasmine woke up to me sitting, looking around the room. *"Time to move,"* she said. Jason got to my place shortly after. It felt like I hadn't seen him in a week. That's what happens when you spend every minute with a person for ten days and they leave for one night.

Today's schedule: Go to the Etobicoke Yacht Club, visit the CN Tower, attend an event called Midnight Madness, and have a nightmare. More than doable. As we drove, a call came in on my headset. It was from a number I didn't recognize.

Voice: *"Hello Mark, I just saw your article on HuffPost. I'm a representative from the new* Meredith Vieira *Show on NBC."*

Me: *"Oh … Hello."*

Voice: *"We think it would be really interesting to have you on the show. I'm an assistant producer here, so I have to pitch you to the big people upstairs, but I was wondering if you'll be in New York anytime soon?"*

Me: *"I could be."*

Voice: *"Your videos are hilarious. This isn't a sure thing, but I wanted to extend my congrats to you and discuss the possibility of a visit soon."*

Me: *"Yes, that sounds wonderful. Thank you."*

Voice: *"I'll send some details to the email on your website and we'll talk soon. Bye for now."*

Me: *"Bye."*

I looked at everyone in the car and promptly began gushing. NBC had just asked me to come to New York City! What was even happening?!

More on that later; back to boating.

We're about to switch between two different Jasons. This might get confusing, and I need your full attention. I'll call Jason D'Souza (my trusty camera man and best friend) Jason D., and Jason Stephanian (sailboat donor) Fredericka. Or Jason S., if that's easier? We arrived at the club and the water was beautiful. Jason S. took us onto the beach and began strapping me into a life jacket. Great, more jackets. He gave me a brief briefing on sailing. On the phone, I'd told him that I didn't really see the humour in sailing. But I was more likely worried I'd fall off the boat.

Somehow, he charmed me onto the dock. I looked around for my boat. Did my boat have racing stripes? Did the sail have racing stripes? All the boats with racing stripes looked intimidating and completely un-sailable to me (I suppose they all did). Then Jason S. directed my attention to our boat. It was the size of a postage stamp. I was starting to see the humour now. I remember getting pretty nervous when he started explaining each safety precaution. There was even a danger of getting knocked out and oh, I don't know, drowning. When the wind shifts, the boon (the metal bar that the sail is attached to) will swing over your head. You have to duck. He explained how to operate the sail, which I'd control with a rope in my mouth, and the rudder, which I'd control with my foot. It all sounded good in theory.

I'll admit that I don't bother learning new skills sometimes because it feels too late (which is somewhat ridiculous, considering I wrote this passage when I was eighteen and will be half-way to thirty by the time it's published). Jason D. had already shown me that this wasn't true. He had learned to operate a camera he knew nothing about in a matter of days, and he was getting better with every video. I took him as an example. If he could become a filmmaker with determination and passion alone,[83] I could learn to sail with foolishness and disregard for procedure.

---

83 He can also juggle now, by the way.

All I needed was double the determination to make up for what I lacked in hands.

We boarded a powerboat and towed the little guy behind us (the boat, not Jason D). I sat back and enjoyed my peaceful voyage to the middle of the lake, watching the water skate by. I closed my eyes, perhaps finally at peace. Jason S. hopped off the big boat into the sailboat and quickly demonstrated how to sail. It seemed like a pretty hand-heavy activity.

Then it was my turn. With some help from everyone on board I got into the sailboat, which was so small I had to sit down. When I imagined sailing, I'd always imagined it standing up. I put the rope in my mouth, propped my foot on the rudder, and tried my damn best. I was floating around the lake aimlessly, but it didn't matter, the shot was stunning. From Etobicoke, we had a perfect view of the Toronto skyline. It was breathtaking.

I guess the skyline was a little too breathtaking, because I didn't notice the bow making its way into the wind. The sail began to swing over and I turned back just in time for the metal boon to hit my already fat lip and knock the rope from my mouth. I doubled over for a second. A loud gasp echoed from the bigger boat. I didn't want to shock anyone, so I sprung back up and shouted, *"I'm good!"* They went back to talking, but I wasn't all that good. My mouth was throbbing, and I could taste blood. That's what happens when you try out your sea legs.[84]

Overall, sailing was a blast. It was a little frustrating, but hey, I was sailing for the first time, with people I loved around me, and a serene skyline to keep me calm. Come to think of it, being in that boat was the first time I'd been alone in eleven days. It hit me like a wave (sorry). I was over the hump.

---

84 Literally.

With the lake air clearing my head, I decided to call it a day. I somehow controlled the boat back to my friends and they managed to pull me on board. I was sitting on the edge of the powerboat when I got stuck. I began to topple overboard, but Jason S.'s dad caught me and pulled me up like a big sack of potatoes. After I steadied myself, we headed back toward the dock.

Jason S. asked me if I wanted my ears swabbed.

"What?" I said.

"Well, they must feel awful after eleven days." Now that was something I hadn't heard yet (sorry).

"Of course, I do." Jason D. began to film while Jason S. swabbed my left ear. It felt good. Most things feel good when you haven't done them in eleven days, actually. We got back to the dock before he had a chance to do my other ear, and so he told me he would do it later.[85]

We met Jasmine near the CN Tower and attempted to go inside. No dice. It was okay. I couldn't really afford the twenty-five-dollar entrance fee anyway. We got a shot of me standing outside of it, so I guess that was the same.[86] There's a huge aquarium next door called Ripley's Aquarium, with a lot of exotic sea creatures. They have everything: regular fish, sharks … that's probably it, actually. It costs thirty dollars to enter. But you get to look at a bunch of water! And fish! Or sharks! The lobby had some fish (or sharks) in open aquariums, so we just hung out there instead and saved our money. I guess today was about giving the impression that we were in a lot of cool places, when in reality we just stood outside of cool places.

There was a big sign in the lobby that read: *"DO NOT PET FISH."* I stuck my whole face over the tank's edge and into the open aquarium. I tried to pet some. Then I ran, unable to wipe the water and fish poop

---

85 He never did.

86 It wasn't.

cocktail from my eyes. Running out of an aquarium dripping wet is a funny visual to me.

Once outside, someone began to approach us. I didn't recognize him at first. He was just a guy rolling a suitcase with something draped over the handlebar. He looked at us, and in a deep growly voice: *"Hey, you're the straitjacket guy."*

I took another look at the handle. It was a Batman costume. The same Batman costume from Dundas Square on day two.

"You never uploaded that picture to my page," he growled.

I tried to explain how busy we were, but he just walked away and shouted, *"Do what it takes!"* We did. It was a very Batman response.

It was getting dark and we still hadn't eaten. Most places in the area were bars, and we were still underage. There was a nicer restaurant near us called Casey's,[87] and so I figured if I was going to have a major expense that day, the least I could do was buy my team dinner.

This was the first day Jason S. had spent with me, and I could tell he was enjoying himself. All of the eyes on us, the whispers; it was exciting! The rest of us were jaded. All that mattered was if those eyes donated. Jasmine had cards on her because she was the organized one and remembered we needed those in public. She gave one to everybody in the restaurant.

Our server was extremely helpful. She offered to help me eat if I needed. Then she winked. Maybe too helpful. Jasmine gripped the fork like a dagger and began feeding me. Jason S. decided to eat without his hands in solidarity. He thought it was a good idea at first, but I watched him slowly change his mind. After we finished, I thanked him for everything. Sailing might have been the most pivotal moment of the stunt. It had brought me out of my slump.

---

87 Since out of business. Again, unrelated to our visit.

TWO WEEKS STRAIT

HOW TO SUCCEED WHEN YOUR HANDS ARE TIED

My mom had agreed to pick us up from the train station and drive us downtown for Midnight Madness, an outdoor social event. We were hell-bent on going. Oakville teenagers could stay out late, buy cotton candy, and drink soda pop. Truly radical. It would be past one a.m. by the time we got there, so hopefully it was still bumping. We made our way to the train and managed to catch one that was leaving right on time. The gentle rock of the car reminded us how sleepy we were.

There she was. Waiting as promised. My mother was outdoing herself. Staying up past midnight is very uncharacteristic of her. She was taking her week "off" seriously. Her motherly instincts were telling her I needed sleep, but her deep mother-intuition knew that this whole thing was bigger than that.

It's times like this when you realize that while your parents can be annoying—and though it should seem totally obvious—no one loves you like they do. My parents have been supportive my whole life, but I can't remember another time when it was this tangible.

It was 12:50 a.m. when we arrived. Fashionably late. We began leisurely walking the streets of downtown Oakville. It gave us all a chance to feel like the teenagers we were again.[88] I looked at Jasmine as we ran up and down the street, ate free popcorn, and sang. There was a local dance school performing salsa outside. I walked into the middle of their dance circle and began spinning around carelessly for the audience that had gathered. When I stopped being able to tell if the laughs felt good, I phoned my mom to bail me out.

We went into the kitchen and my wonderful team poured some hand sanitizer into my arms and wet-napped underneath the jacket. I was morbidly curious about the appearance of my hands. Would they be black due to dirt, or pale from the lack of sun? I'd find out in three days.

---

88 Y'know, if those teenagers are from an affluent white suburb.

Slumped on my mattress now, it was the money I'd promised to raise that was keeping me awake.

DAY 12 - NOTHING MONUMENTAL

(An Affluent White Suburb: Walking to a park in the rain—2014)

JULY 19, 2014: My body was finished. My shoulders were throbbing, everything was clicking, and my stomach was aching. It was probably the combination of poor circulation and lack of sleep. My spirits were high, but my health was declining. Maybe Mom was right.

I woke up at a record-breaking two p.m. Half the day was gone, but we weren't really getting any more suggestions. I knew day thirteen would be interesting, because it was the second last day, but what was so special about day twelve? It didn't help that I just wanted to stay inside at this point. I certainly wasn't in the mood for roller coasters anymore. I hibernated most of the day, watching videos with Jason and Jas. Mostly magic related. Penn and Teller: *Lift Off of Love* (in which they reveal the secrets to sawing-in-half and other big-box illusions); *Animal Traps* (in which they steal food off baited traps); *The Magic Bullet* (in which they catch a bullet between their teeth); *Vanishing a Rabbit* (in which they throw a rabbit into a wood chipper). Then there was David Copperfield: *Flying* (he flies); *Death Saw* (he dies); *Walking Through the Great Wall of China* (what size!). Lance Burton: *Dove Act* (fucking watch this one); *Osmosis* (he appears on a friggin' chandelier); *Sword Fight* (so like, he fights a dude with a sword but then the dude is him? Watch this one too).

I may be blasé with their explanations at this point, but these are the very routines that got me into magic as a kid. And then into a fucking straitjacket twelve years later. I realized Jason was asking more questions about how the videos were shot than about how the magic was done. Perhaps perpetually gripping a camera had exposed his neck to a juicy bite from another type of bug.[89]

Hours flew by. I needed fresh air. I thought going to a park would be entertaining. Monkey bars. Funny. Slides. Funny. But when I went outside

---

89 Foreshadowing. Another rhetorical device I enjoy.

with the gang, we noticed it was raining (because there was water falling from the sky). Meh, the jacket would be fine. I was getting more daring.[90]

We couldn't do much filming on rainy days anyway. Worked for me. The only real suggestion we had was: *"Go on a swing."*

There was a huge puddle of water underneath one of the swings so I, of course, chose that one. I didn't see why swinging would be difficult. Couldn't I just get on and kick my legs back and forth?

I fell off. There I was, tumbling to my doom. I tried to reach out to break my fall, but my arms were (obviously) wrapped in canvas. Got me again! The wind was knocked clean out of me. To make matters worse, the swing chains wrapped around my legs and I was dragged into the puddle. Now the jacket was wet. Insult to injury.

I fell on my right shoulder, and although I couldn't move it properly before the fall, it actually felt better afterward. Maybe chiropractors should start recommending *that* to their patients![91]

Not every day can be monumental. Day twelve was not monumental.

I made two confessionals and fell off a swing. I didn't even have enough content for a daily video. I made the decision to add the strait-jacket footage I'd shot with Scott on day ten. Ironically, day twelve is one of the videos with the most views. I'm pretty sure people just click the video because of the title: *"Guy in straitjacket puts on a straitjacket."*

I couldn't believe it. One day had kind of become the next, and the next, until almost two weeks had passed. I think that's the secret to dealing with most unfavourable moments in life. Fill your day with things you want to

---

90 *Lazy.* I was getting more *lazy.*

91 Or, like, a real doctor.

do no matter how you're feeling. Force yourself to get out there. Time will do the rest. I'd been in the jacket since eight in the morning on July eighth, meaning that at eight a.m. on the twenty-second I'd be finished my two weeks. I was getting so close I could taste it. It could also have been the sweat from around my collar. Anyway, I could taste something.

Jasmine had given up on waiting till Jason fell asleep to join me in bed. We weren't hiding our confusing mess of a relationship anymore. Everyone seemed to understand how complicated it was, and they willingly gave us the space to explore.

As she crawled into my bed that night I said, *"You're going to get your boy back soon, you know?"*[92] Then, like a scene from a movie, she rolled over to face me and said: *"He's right here."*

I looked at the ceiling. *"What are you smiling about?"* she asked. I turned my head toward her.

"I've never felt more free."

---

92 It's unclear even to me if I meant that I'd be myself again or that I wanted to get back together. So, don't ask.

DAY 13 - THE PENULTIMATE DAY

© Personal Collection
(Jason D'Souza)

(Anything for a Laugh: Jason and Jas beg me not to hurt myself on a jungle gym—2014)

JUNE 20, 2014: Big day. I'd raised ten thousand dollars for the foundation, an amazing feat in itself, though still not the goal I'd set for myself. I needed to raise another five thousand—half of what I'd accomplished in thirteen days—in forty-eight hours. The stakes were sky high.

We started the day as all important days should start, with a sugar high. Jason started rolling and we made our way to a popular frozen yogurt place where hip teens could chill.[93] It was one of those self-serve yogurt places where you weigh your yogurt at the end and then promptly take out a loan to pay for it. I went a little apeshit. Luckily, a friend of ours was working and offered to pay. While I was putting toppings on my yogurt, I finally spilled something on the jacket. Chocolate sauce. All over my left arm. I wore it proudly. It took until day thirteen, but I now had a brown stain on the jacket.

After fro-yo, we went back to the park. It was time to get all my last-minute bruises in. I ran directly into the fireman pole, threw my shoulder into the rock climbing wall, and jumped off the structure onto my face. Throwing myself against a jungle gym with my two best friends. I wouldn't have wanted it any other way.

"Will you tackle me?" Not something I usually ask people. But when you get lots of requests to play football in a straitjacket, you play football in a straitjacket. Jason didn't hesitate. What actually happened was less of a tackle and more of a clothesline. From saving my neck, to breaking it.

Shooting that sequence took up a good portion of our day and barely took up a portion of the final video. Most things in show business work that way. We were lucky if an hour of footage got us three seconds of video.

I still had money on the mind. If I didn't meet my original fifteen-thousand-dollar goal, I knew the stunt would forever feel like a failure to me. It wouldn't only feel like I was failing myself, it would feel as if I was failing the community I'd promised to press on for. This project wasn't

---

93 Y'know, if those teenagers are from an affluent … It has since closed down.

I'm only now realizing how many of the places we visited subsequently went out of business. Maybe it did have to do with us.

about goofing off or getting on television: it was about gaining experience, creating relationships with media outlets, and using that exposure to help find a cure for Parkinson's disease.

All of a sudden, I couldn't enjoy playing in the park. I told the team we had to go home.

I don't think leaving at that moment made sense to them. We were having fun. Throughout the two weeks, I was constantly wrestling with this tension. Was the heart of this work the joy of making a positive impact with the friends around me? Or was it executing the stunt to as close to perfect as possible, getting through to as many people as possible, and raising the full amount I'd pledged for the foundation? I think all of the above.

Appreciating the sight of the girl I loved, playing on a jungle gym, while maintaining the scope of what had brought us there in the first place. The people around the world with loved ones suffering or loved ones feeding them. I didn't know how to balance the weight of these things then, but being responsible for balancing them nevertheless taught me what my priorities are, along with who I want to be in relation to the world at large.

We went back to the house to check if we'd missed any suggestions. There was only one from an old fan on YouTube, and it was to eat a s'more.

I couldn't help but wonder, why a s'more? There are messier foods, no? Jason and Jasmine made one using the microwave and filmed me eating it.

"Okay. What next?"

That was sort of it. After the video was edited, I went back and double-checked the suggestion. It clearly read: *"Make a s'more,"* not *eat* a s'more. Me by a campfire melting a marshmallow with a stick in my teeth. Now that would've been funny.

We began planning for our last full day of the stunt. Caroline (one of Scott's friends) had an exciting sports idea, which was funny because I don't know what a "sport" is. I also had to contact a man about borrowing one of his cars. I also had to shower, but that wasn't an option yet.

I stayed up talking with Jasmine and Jason for a while. Jason fell asleep and Jasmine kissed me goodnight. None of us wanted to mention the fact that our little fortress would soon be no more.

DAY 14 - ALL GOOD THINGS

© Personal Collection
(Scott Hammell)

(Team Turbo: Playing soccer in a straitjacket—2014)

JULY 21, 2014: I woke up (thankfully). Jason and I were planning my live escape when a call came through on my headset. A call I didn't need.

Let me preface this by saying that I had the best PR team in the city; they ran my campaign above and beyond the call of duty. The best of the best. This call, however: frustrating (through no fault of their own).

Marion asked if I could speak to the hosts while I was escaping. I said that it would be very difficult and that I'd rather focus on the escape.

"Totally understandable," she said.

She called back within twenty minutes and gave me a rundown.

"Okay Mark, since the producers think it's going to be a little boring to watch you wiggle out of a straitjacket—" Excuse me? *"—they think it makes sense to cut to commercial so you can start the escape. They'll cut back halfway through, and you can throw your jacket off to applause."*

I get paid to perform that boring escape on stage in front of thousands of people, thank you very much. What do they think a straitjacket escape is? Do you think Houdini stepped into a cabinet to do his escape?[94, 95] Marion said that it was what the producers wanted, so I'd have to make it work. I was not happy about it.

"Don't," said Jasmine.

"Don't what?" I said.

"Don't do it." Jasmine was a problem solver. *"Just don't start the escape when they cut to commercial. Start once they say they're live."*

I could just stand there, squirm for a bit, and say something like: *"I have to start my inner concentration."* Then I could escape. Smart.

We had a full list of activities to shoot. It was our last day, after all. Our first brilliant idea was to go to a water park. I would be out of the jacket

---

94 To be fair, yes, he did do that, until he realized that the escape was the entertaining part and promptly threw his cabinet in the trash.

95 He probably didn't throw it in the trash. I didn't know him.

before it had a chance to mold, and it was scorching hot outside. We wanted one of those splash pads that little kids play in. We all got a kick out of that. After boarding the car, my mother drove us to one.

We realized a small flaw in our plan upon arrival. Every parent in town had brought their four-year-old to the splash pad that day to prevent them from overheating. These little bastards were going to ruin our shot.[96] We had to do what was right and not record the toddlers.

"Don't mind me, I'm just going to approach your child in a device used to restrict serial killers in movies. Oh, and do you mind if I film them in the water?"

Tough sell.

We went over to an area that didn't have as many kids. But every time we started shooting, a child would approach, and we'd cut. The water was also on a timed system. We spent a lot of time waiting for it to activate. I had one brilliant moment when all the jets were on and no children were in sight, but Jason forgot to hit record. Nothing made it into the video. Onto our next brilliant idea, the activity thousands of social rejects in small suburban towns flock to: laser tag.

We drove to a Laser Quest we weren't sure was even open, walked in, and launched into our usual routine, but the owner cut us off with: *"Of course!"*

We paid for our game and entered the briefing room, where they put the blue vest over me. Jasmine and Jason were red. I obviously couldn't hold the gun, so we planned to just film me getting "killed" and falling over. Somehow, we didn't account for the fact that it would be pitch black and nearly impossible to record.

Our shots were mostly of a blue smudge in the darkness. So, I forgot about the camera. It was kind of fun. I couldn't be on the offensive, so I kept running around, screaming and diving into hiding spots. The epic music made it all the more enjoyable. We had the whole place to ourselves.

Jason's shoelace came undone, so we stopped for a breather. This is why I didn't wear shoelaces. He started going through footage on the camera,

---

96 I love kids.

so Jasmine bent down to tie his shoe. We were all laughing and panting. Then, the music stopped. Someone entered the space and screamed: *"Hey! What are you doing?!"*

"We're just playing!" I answered.

"That doesn't look like playing!"

Little did I know they had cameras in the playing space, and Jasmine kneeling in front of Jason while out of breath probably didn't look very good. We quickly tried to avoid the awkward conversation and started playing again. He left the space, and we continued to run around. The music didn't come back on. Now it was just the sound of our feet on the wooden floorboards. The sound of shuffling became too much for Jasmine. She ran out to complain about the music. She's pretty persuasive when she's angry. The music was back on within minutes. But the game ended soon after. That was a nice reminder of what it was like to be teenagers. We were doing this great thing for charity and still getting accused of giving blow jobs in a Laser Quest.

Caroline asked her soccer team if I could play with them for a couple of hours. This was a foot-centric game anyway, right? They had *"Team Turbo"* written on these amazing lilac T-shirts, in a font that looked like it had come straight out of Microsoft Paint 2001. I didn't know that I would be playing an actual game against an actual opposing team when I agreed. Okay Team Turbo, it's your funeral.

I also didn't know the mosquitos would be out, and I didn't account for the fact that I wasn't funny anymore. I wasn't that funny to begin with, and now I was tired, grumpy, and uncomfortable. It was time for me to get on stage (field) and perform. Scott took my camera and attached his GoPro to my chest.

I was pushing hard for laughs, pissing off both teams in the process. I should also mention that sports are not my forte.[97] I got into magic for a reason. I met everyone by standing in the net and letting them take free shots on me before the game.

It was fun for a while, but after about fifteen minutes I wanted to be asleep or dead. I was out there to fall down. They were there to win. Some teammates started barking friendly orders at me. Move up, cover your man, rollover. I found it extremely difficult to keep up. Like I was in gym class again. *"I'll be all the way over here, coach! Let me know if the better team needs to be evened out!"*

The first time I fell was genuine. I tripped over somebody's foot while going for the ball. I was going down already anyway, so I made it dramatic. I jumped over the ball and ducked into a roll. As we walked back to our side of the field, I noticed one of my teammates rubbing her face and opening her jaw. Oh god … I'd kicked her in the face. I kicked my fucking teammate in the face. Our editor put it in the video so I would never forget it.

To make matters worse, my falling routine was getting old quick, especially since it was now a hazard. I had a new idea. I would run toward another player and yell at the top of my lungs. That didn't help my likability. New idea! The sympathy card. Fall in front of another player and shout: *"Ow, my leg!"* like soccer players always do. That would be funny and topical, right? I ran for the ball with someone from the opposite team and flung myself in front of him. He kind of hopped over me as I shouted, *"Ow, my leg!"* just like how I'd seen on TV. Apparently, this isn't as funny in a real soccer game, made clear by the whole field going silent and calling a time-out before approaching me. I jumped to my feet.

"Just kidding, I'm fine, hahaha, let's be friends!" or something to that effect. It didn't get a laugh, I'll tell you that. It also made the opposing team like my team less. I played a bit longer and forced some more laughs, until I was asked to swap out for a bit. I never went back on.

---

97 But that is! (Imagine I'm pointing to a KIA Forte.)

The game ended and I went over to apologize to the other team. I thanked them for letting me play. They were good sports about me being not good at sports. I told them about what I was doing, and everyone offered their support. I said goodbye to Team Turbo and tried to hug Caroline. I haven't played soccer since.

On to the adventure of sleeping on Scott's couch. He was driving me to the studio the next morning. He gave me access to everything in his house that I could manage without hands (nothing).

Alex had baked vegan treats, and I was in a happy place before my last straitjacket sleep. Scott said we could drive back to his place after the escape so I could shower and change into respectable clothing.

Scott's house was an oven. No air circulation. The window was shut and I had no arms, but I somehow managed to accomplish three things before getting into bed: One, I used my face to get the window open a crack, two, I kicked the fan on, and three, I, well ...[98]

After we crunched the numbers, I realized we would have twelve thousand dollars raised when I went on the air. Just three thousand dollars shy of my goal. Oh well. Not bad for fourteen days. I tried to bury the final number in my subconscious, refusing to admit that I'd failed. This was my first fundraiser after all, and I needed out. Enough was enough. Plain and simple. It was immense pressure knowing that I had to escape the next day. That was my last thought before drifting off around two-thirty a.m.

---

98 Strummed my banjo.

THE ESCAPE

© Personal Collection
(Scott Hammell)

(The Last Signature—2014)

JULY 22, 2014: Scott shoved me into the car. Barely awake. Alex was coming along to help me look presentable. Good luck. I was beyond incoherent. What nonsense was I going to spew on the air? We were somehow already on the set of *The Morning Show*. Still waking up. We said hello to our friends from two weeks ago. *"Back so soon?"*

They had no idea.

My mom, dad, and Jason were allowed into the studio, along with Scott and Alex. Jasmine was at her series shoot, and Michael waited outside to meet a very important ride from a fellow *Back to the Future* enthusiast.

7.14.14:

I thought I would drop you a line to say awesome stunt! Good luck! And to offer up my DeLorean Time Machine for a photo op or to drop you off at an appearance or something since you're somewhat 'tied down.' Sorry, bad joke.

Wondering how you will reply, both theoretically and literally.

- Ken

Of course, my answer was: *"Oh my fucking god yes please pick me up after my escape in your DeLorean please fuck."* He agreed.[99]

As Michael waited outside, I waited in the greenroom. The monitor caught my eye: *"Famke Janssen after the break."* She looked familiar ... how did I know that name? Then it came to me. James Bond. She was my favourite Bond girl (among other accolades) and here she was, walking on set.

"Excuse me, Miss Janssen?"

She turned around. *"Yes?"*

"Would you sign this straitjacket for charity?"

---

99 Ken and I were complete strangers before this interaction. He reached out after seeing my sorry ass on TV, babbling about Michael J. Fox. What a guy.

She was in a hurry, but she quickly took our sharpie and signed her name nice and big. Last celebrity signature. Last moments in the jacket.

We were next. Scott handed me some protein powder. I downed it as they ushered me into position. A lot of people were moving me around today. *"What's happening? Wait, are we doing this now?"* Suddenly, I was live. I didn't hear another word. I was scanning all of the familiar faces. They said something about how I smelled, and I think I answered. No wait, I didn't. Then we were in commercial. That was my cue. Wake up! I looked at Jason. I started squirming, just like we'd planned, eating into the commercial break. Still scanning the room.

"And we're back!"

What the fuck was happening? Where was my mind? Where was my body? I wasn't entirely sure. It didn't matter. There was no time left. My body took over. Muscle memory and a final rush of adrenaline were all I had now.

JULY 22, 2014: My first out-of-body experience. Throwing myself back and forth. The rigour on my shoulders was excruciating. No time to focus on pain. I started getting dizzy as the clock counted down. One elbow wrenched itself over the other. My right arm snapped over my head. I heard the arm buckle hit the floor. My foot clamped down on it as I swayed back and forth. Jerking back, I peeled the jacket over my head. The smell of rotting flesh consumed me. *I'm going to collapse.* I held my breath. My foot pulling at the sleeves. My head popping out. I slid one hand out, then the other, and watched the jacket hit the floor. My ears were ringing. It was over. I was out.

I completely straightened my arms for the first time in two weeks. The smell filled the studio. My hands were pale and clammy and covered in dead skin. Then the pain. First pins and needles, then numbing in my arms as the blood rushed back into them. Then vomit—vomit coming up my throat. I swallowed, forcing it back down. Wait, oh my god, we're still live. I stumbled around a bit, looked at the hosts and yammered something I hoped was charming. Then I looked at the camera and urged people to continue donating. All of the hosts thanked me, and one was even brave enough to shake my hand. The stunt was over, but we weren't quite done. The DeLorean had arrived. I ran to Jason, who emptied a bottle of hand sanitizer into my palms. I lathered as we ran for the back door. A number of fans and supporters were waiting outside to congratulate us. There was also a huge crowd around the car. It turned out there was a teen beauty pageant happening at the same time in the same place. As they fawned over the real-life time machine, I told them it was my ride. I'm not a big fan of pageants, but I'm a big fan of people who like *Back to the Future.*

The pageant photographer said, *"Alright, now everybody, look at the man and say DAMN!"* They did. He snapped a photo. I've looked better. Once all of the pageant girls had their pictures with the car, it was my turn. We posed as Ken shook my hand. He explained how the car had been overheating all day.[100] I got inside, shut the door, and we sped off into Toronto traffic.

Remembering the pre-stunt pledge by Casey's father, John McMahon, I'd raised $14,500 (so close) and was driving off in my dream car to celebrate. Ken explained that due to the amount I'd raised, the foundation would invite me to an awards dinner with Michael J. Fox in New York City. I just about vomited again.

We circled the block and arrived at the same spot in front of the studio. I hopped out, threw the straitjacket on again (the last thing I wanted to do), and posed for more photos. Ken signed the jacket and drove off.

I should've felt happier, but it was bittersweet. I'd gone on this fourteen-day adventure, and now it was back to life as normal. I hugged my mom and dad. They told me how proud they were. I hugged Scott, and he did the same. I thanked everyone in attendance and said my goodbyes.

Michael, Jason, and I jumped into Scott's car and drove to his place. They laughed the whole way. We were talking about memories from the

---

100 DeLoreans are fickle creatures.

stunt like it had already been five years. I was pointing to places we'd been during the two weeks. Wait. I was pointing. I took a long look at my hands. I texted Jasmine that I missed her. The feeling was mutual.

When we got to Scott's place, I leapt straight for the shower. I scrubbed myself as hard as I could, got out, dried off, and took a whiff. I reeked. I got back in the shower and scrubbed even harder. After my third scrubbing, the smell had mostly come out. I shaved, put on clean clothes, doused myself in cologne, and scratched the entirety of my body. Then I went upstairs and ate a proper meal with a fork and knife. Jason and I juggled together, Scott and I high-fived, Michael and I hugged. I was finally awake.

The first place I went to was Browser's Den,[101] to be around my magic community. Scott dropped us off and went back to his everyday life. He gave me the warmest smile and left. After we bought our tricks, Jason and I said goodbye to Michael and took the train home. We slept the whole way.

When I saw Jasmine again, I almost cried. I squeezed her as hard as I could. I opened my mouth to apologize for my behaviour during the past two weeks.

"Don't," she said.

"Okay ... but I'm really sorry."

We all decided to sleep together[102] at my house one last time, and I was finally able to wrap my arms around her. The nightmares stopped, but I'd be lying if I said I didn't sort of miss my canvas shell.

We weren't the Escaping Parkinson's team anymore. We were just three best friends. We eventually returned to our own homes and

---

101 Toronto's magic store.

102 Like, we slept in the same bed. Like, literally, just slept.

promised each other we would continue to get the most out of each day. We shook on it.

The stunt completely reshaped my body, mind, and soul during a two-week period, but it did much more than that. The straitjacket was off, and so was I.

UNBUCKLED

(Hell's Kitchen: Casey McMahon's apartment in New York City—2015)

8.19.14

WOW COOL. It's done! You're awesome for doing this! It would have been neat if, like the security at Wonderland, some guys in white came and hauled you off to the local asylum. Rubber padded walls you could bounce off of! Seriously, though, you are super awesome. I liked when you tried to hit the punching bag at the gym. The bag seems to punch you instead. lol.

Where can I see you perform? Just in Canada?

You are so cool.

Sorry to question you, what you did was amazing.

- Mike

That's the last I ever heard from Mike and his black leather straitjacket. I'd had my fifteen[103] minutes. I was the straitjacket guy, and then very quickly, I was no one.

Isn't $14,500 just so *painfully* close to our goal? John McMahon thought so, too. He increased his pledge to three thousand dollars in order to push us past our finish line. I breathed a sigh of relief. We had a few donations trickle in during the first week post stunt. $15,635 was the grand total when the Team Fox donation page officially closed. Idea Workshop (our PR team) estimated that thirty-one million people had seen our story worldwide. They continued to insist on donating all their hard work. They wouldn't accept a penny.

Upon weighing me, we discovered that I'd lost eight pounds. *"I should wear a straitjacket for two weeks,"* Jasmine joked.

My body took some getting used to. My arms felt three inches longer, and they seemed cumbersome. I hung up my straitjacket for a year to recover.

---

103 Fourteen.

I felt I had some loose ends to tie up. Like there was this breath caught in my chest that I couldn't exhale.

I started with Wonderland. I had to avenge my previous visit. Michael, Jasmine, and I were going to ride everything if it killed us. We brought Jason this time, too. He was terrified of roller coasters, but I wanted to see how he handled them post stunt. A war on fear had begun. We shared this outlook. It's kind of absurd not to do something because you're scared of the outcome. That's how we get trapped in patterns. I never would have attempted Escaping Parkinson's otherwise.

Security wasn't a problem this time around. I walked up to them.

"Remember me?"

"Couldn't forget. Where's your jacket?"

As far away from me as possible.

After some hyping up, Jason convinced himself to get on the biggest rollercoaster in the park. When we reached the top, he looked at me and said: *"Mark, Dakota!"*[104]

He screamed all the way to the finish but couldn't stop smiling for the rest of the day. I took Jason on as many rides as I could. Either he was a completely different person than when we started off or I was, because I could now confidently call him my best friend. The only thing stopping us from trying anything together was ourselves. If it didn't scare us, it probably wasn't worth doing.

Around six p.m. Michael asked, *"You think we could call it a day?"* I looked at my friends' faces. They were beat. It was time to go home.

Remember that NBC interview I said we'd get back to? We're getting back to it. There wasn't enough time to facilitate a trip before the escape, so it ended up slipping through my fingers. Missed opportunity. However, the foundation invited me to New York City to visit their offices and to

---

104 Our safe word from the two weeks.

show their team some magic. That was more important to me anyway, to be honest.

8.13.14

Hi Mark,

We're excited to have you come to visit!

I'm planning to have a few of my colleagues join us to discuss how things went and to hear what your thoughts were. We'd also like to do some informal filming to share via social media ... would you mind performing a few card tricks that we could share with our community?

I'd also like to gather some thoughts from you for a follow-up blog post, so we can either just talk through or we can do some video recording.

Thanks!

I flew down with my mom in August. I was thrilled to meet the Fox Foundation team that'd made our stunt possible. Kristen and Liz were my saviours during the stunt, and I got to spend some time with them in the offices my hero helped to build. They showed me the back terrace with an absolutely astonishing view of the city. I could tell my mom was proud to be standing there with me. The only person missing was Michael J. Fox himself.

With that, my summer was over, and I was returning to Montreal (I was still completing my post-secondary education, remember?).

Jason and I had grown very close, so I went over to his place to say goodbye. He said he'd made something with my best quote from the stunt on it. A gift? I opened the bag and found a phone case with my picture on it. The quote underneath my face said, *"I like smoothies."* That stupid thing I'd said to Scott on day one. I laughed and thanked him. He always reminded me not to take myself too seriously. Then he started talking about the stunt. About school. About his new outlook on life. About the war on fear. About how he now viewed what he was doing. He'd decided to study business to make a difference, and now it seemed like the furthest thing from different.

"I feel like I accomplished more by filming our antics every day for two weeks than I have since I started business school. I just don't see anything changing here in the next two years."

So, what now?

"Let's work on more stunts," he said. We shook hands.

"Best friends first. Business partners second." Jason has remained a huge part of my life to this day (due to our mutual undying love for art and adventure). We made a difference with a project that set the stage for future schemes. It's a friendship between two committed artists who just can't get enough of the ride. He never gets tired of hearing of my heartbreaks and rollercoaster career moments. He's gentle, kind, and driven. His ambition scares me as much as it motivates me. What more could you ask for in a best friend?

The stunt didn't strengthen every relationship, however. In the immediate aftermath, Jasmine and I spoke about what we were supposed to be. It was clear we both assumed we'd jump back into dating, but it never happened.

I think we tried really hard to be friends at first. And we were. We were the best of friends for a few weeks, maybe a month, but then … Putting your finger on exactly what stops two people from being together can be difficult. An enduring friendship with somebody you were once incredibly intimate with can be even more difficult.

Truly, if you want to know, Jasmine and I were in love. We loved each other. But we were not in a loving relationship. We were in a battle. A battle for power. Always.

We all exhibit toxic traits from time to time. Jasmine and I were explosive. We brought out the worst in each other, each wielding our power in damaging ways. It is not my place to speak for her, but there are certainly things I did that I'm not proud of. I felt my age brought with it a certain wisdom and superiority (I was eighteen and only a year older). I was controlling. I projected my insecurities onto her, forbidding her from doing certain things, as if that was my place at all. I prevented her from distinguishing who she was without me. If Jasmine had realized how intelligent, significant, and powerful she was, I feared she wouldn't want me anymore. I wanted her to look up to me. I longed to be the centre of her world, which inevitably meant minimizing her universe. Nobody deserves to live in the shadow of an ego.

I believe Jasmine helped with Escaping Parkinson's for *me*. I'm not suggesting she wasn't passionate about raising funds for Parkinson's research, but her role in that journey was about supporting me. And she did an incredible job.

I've grown since then—seven years, to be exact. I'm not an eighteen-year-old boy anymore. I'm a man. And I've put in a lot of effort to be one that I'm proud of. I've worked toward no longer being jealous, hot-headed, or self-righteous. I've learned a lot from being treated in ways that I treated Jasmine in subsequent relationships. I still have work to do, but I'm just as motivated to do it as I was to spend two weeks in a straitjacket.

The jacket did a lot of good for a lot of people, but not *all* people. In being blinded by the success of my project, I neglected a few of those around me. I was forced to grapple with the fact that good intentions are not excuses to treat people like shit. "Trying our best" can sometimes allow us to write off despicable behaviour. I learned what being a support-ive partner means to me and the importance of reciprocation. I ultimately lost a friend. For that, I'm still sorry.

Over the years, Jasmine and I have apologized and spoken ourselves numb. In the end, we were two stubborn teenagers who couldn't find the words to say goodbye.

Then again, maybe we did. We've moved on to healthier horizons, proving that everything happened the way it was supposed to. I wish Jasmine the absolute best in life. Things change, and that's okay. Just be sure not to take things for granted or get complacent while you're living them. New opportunities present themselves when you stop clinging to the old ones. You can't move forward by looking back.

NOVEMBER 25, 2014: RecordSetter approved my world record for: "Longest Time Wearing a Straitjacket." I found out from a tweet congratulating me, along with the record in all its glory. There is a little "14 days" sticker under my record on their website. Underneath it is a button that says: "Challenge it!" Yes, go ahead! All you'll need is a straitjacket and two weeks of free time.[105]

> Mark,
>
> Each year Team Fox hosts an Annual MVP Awards Dinner here in NY for our top fundraisers, where Michael is in attendance and enjoys meeting guests. Given your incredible fundraising this year, you have without a doubt earned yourself an invite.
>
> We hope you'll join us in looking forward to April's MVP Dinner!
>
> Let me know your thoughts.
>
> Thanks

My invitation had arrived. Over one hundred of the top donors had been asked to celebrate the seven million dollars raised by Team Fox. I would be flying out to what would soon become my favourite city, to spend time with my favourite people, and meet my biggest hero. If I brought a deck of cards with me, I might even be able to do what I loved.

---

105 This is a serious invitation to break my world record. I'm telling you that I will never do this stunt again. So, go ahead.

APRIL 10, 2015: The day had finally arrived. I was rehearsing for a production of Shakespeare's *Richard III* at school and planning a flight to New York City for the weekend. I was about to receive the best congratulations I could ask for. From a boy planning how to give back to his hero, to a plane ticket, and the opportunity to shake his hand. This was the exhale I needed.

I packed a bag and went to rehearsal.[106] As soon as my last scene finished (and before the play was over) I ran outside. My cab pulled up and I threw my bags into it.

"Pierre Elliott Trudeau airport, please." I rolled down the window and took a deep breath.

Sanjay[107] had agreed to accompany me on the trip. At the risk of making him sound like my ninth choice: Jason was in exams and couldn't get the time off, Scott was tied up with shows, Jasmine and I weren't speaking, Michael didn't have the funds to spend three days in New York (it works out to about five thousand dollars a day), but Sanjay, leader of my high school cohort, was excited and available. He was in Toronto; I was in Montreal. Our planes were scheduled to land at the same time. I boarded and put my headphones in. Peter Gabriel's *"Big Time"* came on. How appropriate. My plane took off down the runway and into the sky. I watched as Montreal grew smaller and smaller behind me.

When Sanjay and I landed in New York, we were in awe at the sheer size and velocity of the city. Sure, I'd just been with my mother, but this was my first time on my own. Casey McMahon[108] let us stay in her apartment while she was away. She had a beautiful place in Hell's Kitchen, and it was ours for three days. We woke up the next morning and took to the

---

106 I hadn't exactly acquired permission to take off on this trip.

107 The launch video shoot manager.

108 Who phoned me at the beginning of this book to become one of our top donors.

streets to film some magic. I was doing anything I could in order to keep myself calm before the big day. We walked around New York, did street magic for strangers, gawked at celebrities, met some new friends, hung out in the opulent apartment, met with the foundation, and ate great food. Only two things were on my mind: How I could move there, and meeting my hero.

I put on my best suit and ran to cocktail hour at the hall. I was greeted with open arms by Liz and Kristen; my Team Fox representatives had become my family now. They hadn't known whether to take my stunt seriously at first, but they ultimately took a chance on it, and that meant so much to me. Kristen told me that Michael was mingling in the hall and I froze up. This could be my only chance. I walked into the ballroom as Sanjay excused himself to the bathroom. I saw someone about twenty feet away with a small group, slowly making his way toward the stage. There he was in the flesh, Michael J. Fox, shaking hands with as many people as he could. Gracious and giving. I walked up, trembling. I could see his warm smile. He was in front of me. I waited patiently for him to notice. I didn't feel like troubling him for a photo. I didn't want him to sign anything. I just wanted to say thank you. His team began ushering him toward the stage and I began to worry that he wouldn't turn around. The moment might escape me. The words leapt out of my mouth.

"*Excuse me, Michael?*" He turned and looked right at me. Then he put his hand out. I'd waited for this moment my whole life. My dream was coming true. I shook it.

"*I worked with your sister Kelli in Toronto!*"

"*Oh, that's great!*"

"*I'm the one who did the stunt.*" His assistant began to remind him of the story.

"*This is the guy who spent that time in a straitjacket, Michael! He's nuts. We thought he was insane, remember?*"

He smiled. "*Yes. Thank you so much for what you did for us.*" He was thanking *me*? His assistant shook my hand and thanked me as well. Then Michael grabbed my lapel.

"Nice suit! You look like a young Bobby Kennedy!"

The speeches were starting, so we said goodbye and he was shown to his table. Four tables ahead of me. I would never be the same after this. I'd just shaken hands with the man who inspired me to act. There were no photos, no videos, no proof. I was sort of disappointed I only had a memory of it, but nevertheless overjoyed that I at least had that.

During the speeches, I was surprised again. Liz gave me a special shout-out. My face came up on screen and everyone cheered. While they were applauding, I began to weep quietly. I had watched Michael J. Fox on screen when I was nine years old and now, nine years later, Michael J. Fox was watching *me* on screen. I thanked them after the speeches, and they asked me if I had any tricks up my sleeve. I must've done magic for every table. It was pouring out of me.

I met the most amazing family: the Achins. We discussed their father, who was also in attendance. He had been diagnosed with Parkinson's and was still fighting. I told everyone I would be more than happy to do magic at any of their events. I wanted to work with the foundation on as many projects as possible. They are some of the most genuine people I have ever met. There was an after-party next door. Sanjay and I managed to get in by slipping through the kitchen and adding to what was already the best night of my life. When it was over, I walked outside into the cool night air and looked down at my palm. I closed my eyes and exhaled.

The next morning, I said my goodbyes to the foundation and the apartment. Sanjay and I made our way to the airport. I filmed him in the cab. He looked at the camera and said, *"To chasing your dreams."*

Then it was back to reality. Back to school. I thanked Sanjay and gave him a huge hug. He grabbed me and said, *"We'll be back soon."*

I wore my suit onto the plane because it made me look like a Kennedy. As I lifted into the sky, I knew. I knew it was the limit. I'd just spent three days in New York City. I'd met people driven toward one collective goal: finding a cure and putting the foundation out of business. That's a business model I can get behind.

When I arrived back in Montreal, a new friend sent me a link. Her message said, *"Looks like you have a photo after all ..."*

(A Dream Come True: Shaking hands with Michael J. Fox—2015)

There was no need to pinch me now.

JULY 8, 2019: I sit here, five years later, in New York City where I now live. Reading over my book and gasping at sections I'd forgotten about, laughing at my unmatched wit. I'm sitting on my balcony at 110th and fifth, looking over the city skyline, reminiscing about when all of this was still a crazy, unattainable dream. Last week, Michael signed the Escaping Parkinson's straitjacket in his home. I just had a meeting with the Team Fox Young Professionals of New York. In two days, I headline at Caroline's on Broadway. Good things happen all at once. But my favourite memories are from before. Before all of this. Before Jason dropped out of business school and became a documentary filmmaker and director of photography. Before he and I went viral[109] for one of our video collaborations. Before we began production together on a series for CBC. Before he moved to New York. Before my partner[110] and I followed … before I was a world record holder. Before I was Mark *Clearview*. When it was just me and my two best friends in a basement. Armed only with our aspirations and persistence. When it was all just a maybe. Those are the memories I'm most fond of. And when I look over this skyline and think back to how I got here, I can pinpoint the exact moment my life shifted into this realm of dreams. I can pinpoint that moment because it exists in these pages.

I'm not so concerned with being the centre of attention these days. When you're constantly asking for an audience, it becomes difficult to discern when you actually deserve one. It cost me a few friendships and prevented me from getting to the root of some creative endeavours. Now, I'd rather work in silence. I'd rather write. I'd rather listen. This way, I can plan deeper projects that reach innumerable people. And when I *do* ask for an audience, you'll know it's something worth watching.

When I started writing this book five years ago, I never thought about how much could change while I worked on it. Tracking my successes, my mistakes, starting a production company with Jason, going through a breakup, finding love again, moving cities … it all informed sections of the writing. My biggest hope is that it inspires or helps you in some way. Who knows where I'll be in another five years? But more importantly, who knows where *you* will be?

People still ask me how I made it through those two weeks. The truth is: you could have too. I'm not special, I'm not superhuman; *I just kept going*. And you've done it before! When you *must* do something, you *will* do something. It's like getting out of bed after a breakup. Your heart is

---

109 Five million views.
110 At the time.

swollen. It feels impossible to carry on with your day, yet somehow, you get out of bed and live. We choose to keep going every day. Straitjacket or not.

Houdini said it better than I ever could:[111]

"I am strong, you see; strong in flesh, but my will has been stronger than my flesh. I have struggled with iron and steel, with locks and chains; I have burned, drowned, and frozen till my body has become almost insensible to pain; I have done things which rightly I could not do, because I said to myself, 'You must.'"

- Mark Clearview
(the only)

---

111 Kalush, William and Larry Sloman. *The Secret Life of Houdini.* Atria Books, 2007.

A NOTE ON THE PANDEMIC

OCTOBER 28, 2021: Rewriting this book during such a life-changing time has been both eye-opening and affirming. Life has evolved plenty since that final passage. New friends, television, appearances, DeLorean ownership ... but I am often reminded of my experience in the jacket through these isolating times. When I couldn't shake anyone's hand. When I felt trapped. I am reminded that I bumped elbows as a greeting before it was cool. These past two years have been incredibly challenging and incredibly healing (I have the privilege of reflecting in this way, knowing that many have not been so lucky in the face of the virus). I think, now more than ever, we should remind ourselves what we're capable of with a little perseverance and a healthy dose of perspective.

When I got down on myself for being sluggish through 2020, I reread my last piece of writing from July 2019:

*"Who knows where I'll be in another five years? But more importantly, who knows where **you** will be?"*

Of course, I could never have predicted how prescient these words would seem. Only not for five years into the future, but a mere eight months later. And better still:

*"People still ask me how I made it through those two weeks. The truth is: you could have too. I'm not special, I'm not superhuman; **I just kept going.**"*

Damn I'm good.

Things change, and that's okay. It isn't how much we accomplish in any given year that matters. It's about the lessons we learn along the way.

And boy did we learn a lot.

HUGE ACKNOWLEDGMENTS

FEBRUARY 22, 2022: I'd like to thank the following people for their help, support, and donations. Without these people, I would not be writing this sentence. I also wouldn't be the person I am today. I might not exist at all, actually.

Those currently battling Parkinson's disease, thank you deeply. The success of this stunt lives with you, not me.

Everyone who donated. Especially if your name is on that straitjacket. That is never going away. You all surprised me so much. The fact that I was able to raise over fifteen thousand dollars with my first fundraiser is unreal. I thank all of you from the bottom of my heart.

Everyone who tuned in. As we all know, views are the biggest indicator of support these days. The daily vlogs amassed a collective two hundred thousand views.

Jasmine Harper. You did so much you didn't have to. It was not a fun two weeks, but you still held me and fed me. Nothing will take away from the memories I made with you and the time we spent together. You changed me in ways I never could've prepared for. For that, I thank you.

Mom and Dad. One: because you're my parents, and two: because you're already mad for not being mentioned first. You made me, after all! I hope you're proud of what came out. You're two of the most supportive people on the planet, and bonus points for not fucking me up *too* bad when I was a child. Mom, you always made sure I had everything I needed to follow my dreams. Dad, you drove me to my shows and built my props when I was a kid-magician. You two never stopped believing in me (no matter how many of my teachers told you to). Thanks Mom, I love you. Thanks Dad, you are missed around here. I love you.

Jason D'Souza. For continuing to be my best friend first, and business partner second. We've created so much together, and it doesn't stop here. I can always go to you with crazy ideas. I can't wait to see what continue to create together. I love you to pieces and I will change the world with you. Just wait.

Scott Hammell. Without you, I'd have no career. You put me where I am today! You're the greatest person I know, and I'm so lucky to be able to count on you. You're stupid talented. I love you dearly, and if I ever planned a successful project, you were probably the first one to hear about it.

Karleena Kelly. For putting up with me while I wrote this book. It was a pleasure sharing three years with you. You were very understanding of all the reminiscing and soul searching I had to do while editing this. I'm lucky to have found an even richer chapter of my life in you. You're strong, smart, and supportive, and I wish you great success in whatever you set your mind to. I'll never regret loving you. Thank you for everything.

Kelli Fox. For acting with me in my first professional production and being one of the sweetest women I have worked with to date. If it wasn't for you, this stunt would've turned out very differently. Thank you for staying involved, Kelli.

Susan Cohen. For doing more physical work on the stunt than anyone else. You designed the website (twice!) perfectly. You were too kind to me when I continued to give you problems. I owe all of the online traction to you. I also owe you for many morning pancakes.

Rosemary Reid. For working alone on the stunt for a long time. You were on board before the stunt offered any rewards, and that's huge. You did all the writing, making everything sound ten times more professional than I ever could. Then you read and reviewed a very rough manuscript. If my writing doesn't sound good, who's going to believe in me?

Erik Berg. For keeping me sane when I lost my mind at school. We speak the same language. We both want to make art, destroy capital, and help people (those last two are the same thing). The way you live inspires others to live. You were the first one to read this book (and edit it). Couldn't have done it without you.

Max Litzgus. For being the best film editor I could've asked for. You did everything for next to nothing (nothing) and made the people watching want more. The success of every daily video is due to all your hard work.

Michael J. Fox. For inspiring the whole stunt. What you've done with what you've been handed is unbelievable. If I can live a life that mirrors yours in any capacity, I don't see how that could be a bad thing. Thank you for thanking me, and thank you for taking the time to shake my hand.

Cynapsus Therapeutics. For the size of your donation. That one really pushed us over the edge.

The McMahon Family. For your huge donation. The stunt became sustainable when you stepped onboard. Thank you.

Jo-Anne and Jon Packer. For propelling this project to international status, and for donating your services. Without you we would not have those thirty-one million media impressions. I also probably wouldn't have met my hero. Thank you.

Adam Bovoletis, Joseph Milando, and Mark Belsky. For filming the original promo video. If it wasn't so watchable, we would've been in trouble.

Michael MacLaren. For doing one too many things only Michael MacLaren would be willing to do. You're one of my best friends in the whole world. You helped me survive high school.

Liz. For organizing everything in New York. Thank you, Liz, for taking a chance on a teenager with an odd idea. Thank you for the shout-out. Thank you for everything you do for the Parkinson's community.

Kristen. Thank you for everything you're doing with the foundation. Thank you for the support. Canadians represent.

Eliza Bronte. For your support. You've helped coach me through some pretty confusing times in my life. Thank you.

Adriana Bogaard. For keeping me honest. Your support came when I needed it the most. When the stunt was a story of the past. When I tried to write a book about it while being a full-time student. When it didn't matter anymore. You also edited the entire manuscript. You've stuck by my side through years of missteps. I love you.

John and Rachel Correia. For your amazing donation to my publicity and design. Without that first cheque I never would've gotten this stunt off the ground. You have always been so supportive.

Madelyn Keys. For your help finishing this book. You originally agreed to help me copy edit and slowly became one of the best content editors I have ever worked with. I kept saying, *"Okay just work this section … okay, and this section … oh, and this one."* You're just so good. This book sounds good because of you. Thank you.

Juliann Garisto. For your fierce work as a copy editor. Not one single task was too big for you. Through late night messages and early morning phone calls, you were able to handle my energy and edit my book with care. Thank you.

Sanjay Parker. For managing the original shoot, for managing me, and for years of friendship.

Aaron Fisher. For helping me cope with the aftermath, and for becoming a mentor. Thank you for all your advice and thank you for all the laughs.

Lee Asher. For all of your advice on the media. If it wasn't for an early conversation with you, I would've blown my entire plan for exposure.

I'd also like to thank:
Mark Sommerfeld, for letting us use your space.
Milena Vujanovic, for the graphic design that made me look good.
Wing-Kei at One Stop Print Shop, for all the print.
Jake Feeney, for helping me roof.
Nick Van DoeSelaar, for producing the music we used in the promo video.
Brandon James, for the cover design.
Wayne Houchin, for all of your pre-stunt advice.
Ken Kapalowski, for your time machine.

Of course, a huge thank you to our corporate sponsors:
BarHaven Limited/McDonald's Canada
Pet Smart
Eckler Limited

And one last thank you to the Michael J. Fox Foundation, Mina DiDomenico, Peewee and Teewee, Nina Tringali, Eric Leclerc, Marion Morris, Shawn Farquhar, the Etobicoke School of the Arts, Juliette Goglia, the Achin family, Rachael Ruth, Sarah Soloman, Heidi Doorfmeister, Jackie Patrick, the Team Fox Young Professionals of NYC, Virginie Morin-Laporte, Susan Bourne, Jesse Philippe, Jason Stephanian, David Latham, Attila Kadar, Darren Black, Ben Sutherland, Doug Ennenberg, Jason Rice, Alexandra Moye, Howard, Caroline Pandeli, Chesney-Jané Skinner, aunt Mary, Alex and Sebastien at Barbare, Ben Mulroney, Famke Janssen, Bret Parker, Melissa Derfler, Jivan Gandhi, Kirsten Neprily, Christopher Lynch, Chrissy Swehla, David Klein, Sura Mallouh, Sara Garisto, Janel Rae Filipiak, Jonathan Vickburg, Mike Post, Justin at Wells Auto, Hannah Ciordas, Jonah Babins, Mike and Jen Segal, Tansy, and anyone else I'm forgetting.

Lastly, I want to thank you for reading this book. Now go do something crazy. Drop out of school! Confess your love for someone! Quit your job! (I wouldn't recommend the straitjacket thing.)

ABOUT THE AUTHOR

Mark Clearview is a magician, comedian, actor, producer, and now, author (a master of none). He splits his time between Toronto and New York City, performing regularly at the hottest venues in Manhattan; as well as Las Vegas, Qatar, France, Singapore, and China. His clientele ranges from celebrities to high-profile executives at Google, Nestlé, and other mega-conglomerates. Cool! Clearview frequently headlines the illustrious *Caroline's on Broadway* in the heart of Times Square. He was also the resident magician at the acclaimed Michelin star restaurant the *Musket Room*, The Edition Hotel's *Paradise Club*, and the popular speakeasy *Bathtub Gin*. He also frequents *The Magic Castle* in Los Angeles, CA. Clearview has been showcased on countless television networks worldwide. He was featured on Season 8 of *Penn & Teller: Fool Us*. He was the magic consultant and hand-double for Hallmark Channel's *Good Witch*. He wrote, produced, and starred in a nine-sketch series for CBC Comedy. He gained over half a million views on YouTube and over fifty million views on Facebook with his *Noodle Boys* viral videos.

The story of Escaping Parkinson's has also been presented as a TEDx Talk. More information can be found at markclearview.com.

© Jason D'Souza